choose your own disaster

choose your own disaster

A. a memoir
B. a personality quiz
C. a mostly true and
   completely honest look
   at one young woman's
   attempt to find herself
D. all of the above

Dana Schwartz

GRAND CENTRAL
PUBLISHING
New York Boston

Grand Central Publishing
Hachette Book Group
1290 Avenue of the Americas, New York, NY 10104
grandcentralpublishing.com
twitter.com/grandcentralpub

First Edition: June 2018

Grand Central Publishing is a division of Hachette Book Group, Inc. The Grand Central Publishing name and logo is a trademark of Hachette Book Group, Inc.

The publisher is not responsible for websites (or their content) that are not owned by the publisher.

The Hachette Speakers Bureau provides a wide range of authors for speaking events. To find out more, go to www.hachettespeakersbureau.com or call (866) 376-6591.

LCCN: 2018932213
ISBNs: 978-1-4789-7039-2 (trade paperback), 978-1-4789-7038-5 (ebook)

Printed in the United States of America

LSC-C

10 9 8 7 6 5 4 3 2 1

To my family. Please don't read this.

I had considered how the things that never happen, are often as much realities to us, in their effects, as those that are accomplished.

—Charles Dickens, *David Copperfield*

The unpredictable and the predetermined unfold together to make everything the way it is.

—Tom Stoppard, *Arcadia*

choose your own disaster

WHICH FAKE ROM-COM LADY CAREER SHOULD YOU PURSUE?

1. Are you a left-brain thinker or a right-brain thinker?

A. Left brain

B. Right brain

2. What was your favorite subject in school?

A. English

B. Biology

3. Would you rather be fulfilled or rich?

A. Fulfilled

B. Rich

4. In sixth grade, you read *The Call of the Wild* and your English teacher has you create a project to represent the book. You would prefer to:

A. Draw a wolf with charcoal and place a poem you wrote and printed onto clear paper over the drawing for an effect that you truly think belongs in an art museum.

B. Build a small model sled out of wood.

5. On a winter day in the sixth grade, your same English teacher—a woman with a poodle poof of white hair, who wears floor-length skirts and a brooch at her neck like she's onboard the *Titanic*—comes outside to shepherd you back in from recess when she slips on the ice. But not just "slip" the way most people use the word *slip*. She slips like a cartoon character, tiny-heeled boots flung straight out in front of her so she's fully horizontal above the ground before she falls. "I'm okay!" she croaks from the pavement. Do you laugh? Please note here that she is actually completely uninjured. Promise.

A. Of course you laugh. You're not proud of it, but what do you want me to say here?

B. No. I mean, yes, but you're going to say no because even though it said she wasn't hurt, this might turn out to be a trick question or something.

If you answered mostly As

Congratulations! Your rom-com lady career is vaguely arts related, probably at a television studio or women's magazine. If the former, you'll be wearing a headset microphone and carrying a clipboard, flitting around a control room in a pencil skirt and high heels. If the latter, you'll be carrying a half dozen coffees that are spilling all over your cardigan, flitting around New York City in a pencil skirt and high heels. Being clumsy is your primary—and adorable—character trait. Your apartment is inexplicably massive and your wardrobe is all designer blazers and statement jackets in bright colors, and even though they should all be covered in coffee all the time, on account of all the coffee you spill, they always look perfect. You will never get persnickety emails from your bank account, heavy with electronic red exclamation points, about overdraft fees and you will never, ever be sitting barefoot on your couch and feel a slight tickle and look down to see a cockroach the size of a baseball, all legs and hair-thin quivering antennae, crawling across your foot and disappearing beneath the oven before you have a chance to kill it, so you just have to know, forever, that that giant cockroach is living somewhere in your house, waiting to emerge, and it's already gotten a taste for crawling across human flesh. No. Your apartment is always spotless, and your hair is always professionally blown out.

Turn to page 18.

If you answered mostly Bs

You should be the love interest in an action movie. Think Bond girl—you're incredibly smart in the one specific area that just so happens to help the protagonist in this one very specific instant of the plot. "Give me that," you'll say, snatching the hieroglyph from the hero's hand. "I have two PhDs in cryptozoological translation." You'll shove the hero aside from the beeping machine. "I'm NASA's top-ranking expert in nuclear disarmament techniques." Does it make sense? No, but who cares? You are very, very pretty. And smart, definitely smart because even though you look like a supermodel and wear very sexy clothing and a full face of makeup, you are *also* wearing glasses. Sure, twenty-four looks a little young to have three PhDs but they're pretty sure making you smart in whatever will move the plot forward means this movie is feminist. You will either end up running away with the hero, or you will die. Apologies.

Turn to page 5.

HERE IS HOW YOU CUT OFF A MOUSE'S TAIL:

Step 1: Get an internship at the laboratory in the biology building at the center of campus. The animal labs are all several floors down, below the concrete and perfectly manicured grass squares. Your first time walking through the industrial hallways, you'll pass doors guarding pigs and mice (you've heard that there are also primates somewhere in the underground labyrinth of hallways, but their location—and existence—was classified after a legion of animal rights activists in the 1970s engineered a plot to set them free).

Step 2: Get dressed. You'll never quite be sure whether the protective gear you have to wear when you enter the room with the cages is for your protection or that of the mice, with their delicate, scientifically coordinated immune systems. It will take you five full minutes to pull on the covers for your shoes, the gloves, the hair net, and the thin plastic apron while your new supervisor watches, teaching you how to make sure the elastic is all the way around your shoes and making you promise you will never touch a doorknob with a gloved hand. (Is it to keep whatever bacteria you're playing with off the doorknob or to make sure you don't contaminate your experiment?)

"Today, we're going to be snipping their tails for PCR samples," your supervisor says, swiping her access card to get you into the mouse room. She's about forty-five years old, with shoulder-length hair like Kathy Bates in *Misery*. She's just a technician, not the scientist in charge of the lab. Among the many things she's told you that you don't quite understand, you don't entirely know what PCR stands for. "Eventually you'll be doing this on your own, but it takes some getting used to," she continues.

The mouse room is about the size of a prison cell, lined on all sides with stacked plastic cages, each filled with its own generation of mice, their unique genetic and pharmaceutical history carefully marked on an identifying card. The smell is exactly how you'd imagine it, and just a little worse.

The lab tech grabs one of the plastic cages and brings it over to a laboratory hood—stainless steel and connected through the ceiling to a chimney on the roof, like a hood that you would find above the stove in a sinister, science-fiction-villain kitchen—with a thin moat of mesh wiring bordering the table. The moat, it turns out, is the most humane mouse trap you've ever seen: The lab tech expertly extracts a chosen mouse from its plastic habitat and places it on the mesh, where its tiny mouse claws are so occupied with gripping tight to the wiring that it somehow finds itself incapable of moving.

"We're not cutting off the whole tail, obviously, just enough to get a genetic sample," she says out the side of her mouth. Somehow, even with the stench of the mouse shit and the few feet of space between the two of you, you can smell her warm peanut butter breath.

Step 3: Pick the mouse up from its mesh-wire paralysis using your left hand, so it is belly-up in your palm. Using your thumb and index finger, restrain its top two legs. Using your ring finger, hold down its lower torso. You will use your pinkie to hold the tail stable while you take the small silver scissors and snip off less than a centimeter of flesh from the end of the tail.

It somehow seems so much more awful that you have to use a pair of scissors. As if you're a sadistic future sociopath at home with the family pet. The mouse does not squeak, and you are told that it doesn't hurt. There is rarely more than a drop of blood, and you dab it away easily with a delicate tissue Kimwipe. The tail sample goes into a small bullet-shaped plastic tube and the mouse goes back into the box after one final step.

Step 4: This is the most important step. Don't disappoint the advisor who got you this job, the man who wrote the email and gave you glowing praise that you didn't deserve, about how brilliant and hardworking you are. You always looked forward to your freshman advisor meetings with him: ten minutes that turned into fifteen that turned into twenty in his office, which was bedecked with *Star Trek* memorabilia and close-up black-and-white photos of the parasitic worm he discovered that made him renowned in the biology community. When you told him you were planning on becoming a doctor, he was thrilled. "You're one of the good ones," he said conspiratorially, indicating that he had just ushered one of the bad ones out of a previous meeting. The bad ones were the stereotypical premeds—hyper-competitive, type A, their lives planned out down to their residency hospitals and what color scrubs they'll wear when they get there. "You *should* be a doctor," your advisor tells you, offering you a bowl of Hershey's Kisses. "We need more doctors like you." You decline; he pops two in his mouth. You aren't sure how you were able to trick him so completely.

And now you're here, your first day, in one of the best labs on campus.

Try to do a good job.

"Oh, and when you're piercing the ear, you have to fold the ear in half, like this. If you pierce it through without folding it, the mice can just rip the tag right out. So here, look." The lab tech demonstrates for you, folding one mouse's velvety ear within the metal fingers of the handheld gun and then depressing the trigger.

Piercing a mouse's folded ear, you discover, is infinitely more unpleasant than using scissors to snip its tail. The ear is so velvety soft, it seems, and delicate, and you can feel the crunch of the cartilage in your hand as you push the thick needle and plastic marker through. There is no blood and no cries of pain, but you feel as though this is the part that hurts the mouse the most.

"So you'll just finish up with the rest of this group," the lab tech says, and she heads back toward the main laboratory, leaving you alone in a glorified closet, surrounded by rodents and their smell, working under fluorescent lights that still manage to leave the room too dark. "Oh, and remind me to grab you the independent study application when we're back upstairs. The doctor likes to plan ahead about what her interns will be writing their senior theses on."

You have no idea what you'll be writing your senior thesis on. You aren't sure what this lab is actually studying. Liver cancer or something. You managed to trick them in your interview too. They saw the recommendation from your advisor and your good grades and figured any bio major at Brown is as good as the next. You wish you could wear a shirt that says "I missed the day where they explained everything." Which lecture was it exactly, what class, what moment, what point studying for what test did you stop understanding and begin pretending you did? You're planning on just pretending you understand all the way through your medical school applications. Once you're at med school, it's day one for everyone. Just study the textbook and become a doctor.

Follow the steps.

You try to grab your first mouse, and it wriggles away from your grip. The mouse burrows itself into the wood shavings. And so you try to grab another mouse, one that looks almost sedate, sitting on a pile of wood shavings like a proud, fat king. But the moment you get the mouse king in your left hand, it begins violently shaking like a teenager at a metal concert, fighting desperately to escape your grasp, little pink feet crawling on the air, head shaking back and forth—*you can't tell me what to do, Mom!*

You're forced to drop the mouse back onto the metal grating twice so you can readjust your hand position before you manage to get that scissor snip of the tail tip. Once that bit of its DNA is gone, the mouse loses most of its will to fight. It allows you to fold and pierce its ear with only your own squeamishness to overcome.

You never thought you were a squeamish person before. You fantasize about plucking ingrown hairs and, unlike your younger sister who shrieked and cried, even well into teenager years, when faced with the prospect of getting a shot, you never minded needles or blood.

But using scissors to snip a piece of living flesh is harder than you imagined, and it doesn't get easier, not after the first mouse, or the third or the tenth. Using the thick metal gun, closer to a hole punch than anything else, to brutalize through two layers of ear will still make you cringe years later.

The first mouse is done. You are now alone but for a hundred mice in a dark basement room. And you have a dozen mice to cut and pierce before you can leave. Trying to become a doctor is lonelier than you expected.

From kindergarten on, when the inevitable question of "What do you want to be when you grow up?" came, you always had an answer that matched the inflated sense of self-worth of a white girl in an upper-middle-class family in an upper-middle-class suburb, who has been told over and over again that she can achieve anything she puts her mind to. When someone asks this question, they're not just asking about jobs—children don't really understand the fundamentals of jobs: the daily rigor, the monotony, the paperwork, the busywork, the struggling, the interviewing, the promotions, and so on—they're asking them about their future. "Who do you want to be, child?" they ask. The child's answer is inevitably one of the primary-colored figures they've seen waving from the pages of picture books or from *Sesame Street*: Susan is a dancer—see Susan in her tutu onstage at the big city ballet show? Tamako is a doctor—Tamako will be in a white coat with a stethoscope around her neck. Do you want to be a dancer or a doctor or a lawyer or a teacher or a businessperson or a firefighter or a policeperson?

There are an infinite number of careers you can have, and when we say *infinite* we mean about eight. Your job will not just be your job—it will be the very thing you *are*. It will be how you are introduced when you're standing alongside your improbably international and diverse friends in the coloring book. The job itself will be your costume.

And so, from an early age you knew: You didn't just want a job; you wanted an identity. "First female president" was the answer you stuck to from second grade. You believed it with such earnest naivety that you looked upon Hillary Clinton as a competitive colleague. "Talk show host" was another popular contender: Your mother watched *Oprah* every day when you came home from school, and so you watched *Oprah* every day when you came home from school. You pictured yourself holding court every weekday with celebrity guests and politicians, involved and respected, in a job that seemed to mainly consist of talking, using luxury products, and being cheered for. You entertained dozens of fantasies of careers upon which you might embark, from evolutionary biologist like Jane Goodall to celebrity chef, and although they seemed unrelated, they were tied together by an obvious unifying factor: You wanted to be respected, and you wanted to be known. The nightmare for you was never death; the nightmare was being forced to live your entire life anonymous to the people who mattered. You wanted to be a part of the action, and a part of the action in a way that people respected your opinion.

Maybe that's why, as you grew older and you realized becoming president requires a lot of money and handshaking and paperwork and that to be a celebrity chef one needs to be good at cooking, you gravitated toward science.

Science is wonderful if you enjoy feeling smart. "Monosaccharides," you can say, nodding your head thoughtfully. "Cis isomer. *Ardipithecus ramidus.* Gel electrophoresis. Saltatory conduction." And suddenly the world will be filled with people entranced by your genius, totally aware of how smart you are and how much they should respect your opinion, even on things you received B minuses on in tests. And imagine how much greater that feeling will be once you have

Dr. in front of your name. "What does your daughter do?" people will ask your mother in the grocery store. "Oh," your mom will say, trying to conceal a smile, "she's a doctor."

"I always knew she was smart," the stranger will reply, validating your years of schooling and thousands of dollars of debt from miles away.

It's easy. Well, not always easy in practice (you still have nightmares about diagrams in organic chemistry, sloppy lines facing the wrong way, cramped notes taken in a foreign language of which you haven't yet grasped the grammar), but at least the path forward is clear. That's the terrifying thing about adulthood, right? Leaving the tributary river of childhood in which progress is so clearly prescribed along a narrow to-do list—high school, college, internships, good grades—and then spilling out into a massive ocean. But being a doctor has steps: You get internships in laboratories; you volunteer with patients; you take organic chemistry and study for the MCAT and apply for medical school. And then it's three years of school and then an internship and then a residency and by then you'll be a bona fide adult, most likely with an apartment where you live with a cat and a significant other and you will have a job. You will be a doctor and you will be respected.

As soon as you settle on the plan in your mind, you feel as though you might as well be comatose for the next ten years. You wish you could skip ahead. In knowing exactly what you're going to do, you might as well have already done it. Is there any way to get the acclaim and recognition of being an internationally famous and wealthy doctor who is universally renowned as an expert in her field without having to work really hard and figure out if you're actually good enough? Isn't there just a way to skip all of the school and the studying and the proving yourself and the anonymity and coast to mind-boggling success based on potential alone? It's as if the System somehow seems entirely indifferent to the fact that your parents called you gifted as a child.

So for now you're alone, in a room in the cold fluorescent hallways of a biology lab three floors beneath a neo-brutalist concrete building, and you have three more plastic crates, each filled with a litter of mice, to go through, snipping tails and mutilating ears. It will be a few hours before you see another human again. You know, somehow, that the research you're obliquely facilitating is going to help people someday, or at least will disprove someone's idea of something that might have helped people someday. But right now, in this basement room in the cold fluorescent hallways of a biology lab, it doesn't feel like you're doing anything useful.

One day, when you have time and the light is just right and you've already eaten breakfast and done yoga (you're the type of person who does yoga now), you'll spend a full day reading every single scientific paper that's been produced about lab mice and cancer until you're an expert in the field. It doesn't matter that every paper you've attempted to read thus far has become gibberish by the first sentence—in this morning/yoga fantasy, you understand every word even better than the author. You actually get to mail snooty letters to the editor about minor mistakes. That's how well you understand it.

Someday you'll have a lab of your own filled with exotic specimens flown in from other labs all over the country and you'll know what to do with them. You'll have your own undergraduate student alone in a room on her first day, snipping off mouse tails and trying her best not to get scratched. You just have to stick to the path.

As you finish disfiguring a particularly fidgety mouse and recognize that you still have half a dozen left to go, a particularly insidious thought floats into your head: You don't have to come back to the lab tomorrow. That tiny realization blooms in your brain like a rosebud submerged in water. There's no reason you have to work in this lab now, as a sophomore, not really. You can send an email to the head of the laboratory saying you were wrong, you're sorry but you're too busy with schoolwork and you just don't think it's a good fit. You are staring down a long year of hours spent using pipettes and PCR machines and making careful notes and keeping track of how many mouse babies are born and how many are male and how many are female and how many were eaten by the mother because, yes, you learn, that does happen.

You are staring down your entire future, but you don't have to be.

Do you continue to work in the mouse lab?

A. Yes. Even though today it's just cutting tails and tagging ears, in a few years your life will be just like *Grey's Anatomy*—you'll wear scrubs that inexplicably still make your butt look cute and you'll hook up with the other cute-butted doctors in the break room in between lifesaving procedures that end with families in tears hugging you for your incredible work. (You haven't actually seen *Grey's Anatomy*.) You'll win awards and walk in clacking heels down hospital hallways and get called brilliant. All you need to do is follow the right steps.

Turn to page 16.

B. No. There's a reason you don't really know what you're doing, because this isn't what you're *supposed* to be doing. You're far too creative and funny to be wasting your life in the back room of a basement laboratory. You've never been that meticulous or organized either, and when you're a doctor, that will probably lead to accidentally killing a bunch of people. You're smart; you can find something else to succeed at that doesn't take about fifteen years and $150,000.

Turn to page 18.

YOU ARE BECOMING A DOCTOR. Good! That feels right. You are so proud every time you go to the grocery store with your mother on weekends back in the suburb you grew up in. "What are you up to?" the mother of a high school classmate asks, her purse jangling against her grocery cart filled with SmartPop!

You give a practiced shrug of modesty. "Well, I'm a senior at Brown now and applying for med school."

Your mom interrupts here. "She's already been offered a spot at [Harvard/Yale/Penn/UChicago]," she says, beaming.

Remember all of those doubts you had? How you felt as though you were always on your back foot, and any internship or lab position or good grade you received was granted only by luck and trickery? Well, you must have been wrong, because now you're going to be a doctor. If you ever doubted you were smart enough, well doubt no more. All you need to do is follow along the instructions on this path as they're given and you will be a Success.

And eventually, you are. You like what you do—you're helping people every day, and you're on your feet, running through the squeaking white linoleum hallways of hospital buildings and you get to tell people what to do and make small incisions in flesh and sew up bodies like they're the halter tops you made out of bandanas when you were in seventh grade. You're good at your job, and people thank you for it. You are Dr. Schwartz and people respect your opinion and entrust their vulnerable, mortal flesh into your care.

When your children have finally made it off to college,

you buy a nice cabin in Vail (you ski in this future) with your husband Ari or David or Jonathan or Adam, and you wear Lululemon pants every day and have sex when you can stomach it, and you buy a nice purse for yourself on your birthday, and you take vacations. You collect the mementos of upper-middle-class life one by one and you tell yourself, sure, being a doctor is a lot of paperwork, and Ari or David or Jonathan or Adam is losing his hair, and there will always be someone skinnier than you, and did you hear that Jenna—you know, Jenna from high school—actually works as a producer on SNL now? and people are just a little more jealous of her and her glamorous life, but you are a doctor, and you make a good living, and you have a family, and maybe you don't really save lives anymore because you're a dermatologist, but you did catch that mole the other week, and you are content doing this professional, worthwhile thing that impresses people and you are happy. Or at least, happy most of the time. What is being happy anyway? It's the few moments you have to yourself, in the quiet while you're brushing your teeth or folding laundry when you realize you have a good job and a good family and enough money to get by and to appreciate it. So, yes, you think. You're happy.

THE END

Or go back to page 14.

WHAT SORT OF WRITER
WILL YOU BECOME?

1. When someone asks you what your favorite book is, what will you say?

A. *The Crying of Lot 49*. You would say *Gravity's Rainbow*, but you haven't exactly finished it yet even though you keep it in a very prominent spot on your bedside table.

B. You tell the truth: *Ender's Game*, the book you read when you were in fifth grade. It was the first book that seemed to speak directly to you, to understand you in a way no other book, or even person, had ever understood you before. Ender, like you, was the third child—brilliant but lonely, better at things than older kids but caught between the desire to show off and the need to avoid bullying. The ending of the book, so maudlin and condescending to your current cynical twenty-four-year-old mind, was perfect when you were twelve. It was heartbreaking and as fragile as the ice that crystallized over a puddle, waiting for someone to crack it with their boot. Years later, you would find out that its author, Orson Scott Card, is a homophobe and bigot, an entrenched, angry old man who stands against everything you believe, and you'll feel almost violated with how easily he had slipped into your child-brain. He was a terrible person, and he understood you completely in a way that you felt your parents would never be able to. You don't like telling people *Ender's Game* is your favorite book anymore. Sometimes you say *The Martian Chronicles*, a book by Ray Bradbury you read in seventh grade that left you with the same sense of delicious heartbreak when you finished it.

C. Proust, in the original French. It changed your life, but you're not such an asshole that you tell people that you read it in French.

2. What do you eat for breakfast?

A. Black coffee, with a side of a half pack of cigarettes.

B. You usually don't. But if you're only running an hour late for work, rather than your typical two, you'll spend $7.00 on a latte and croissant at the chain coffee place around the corner from your office. Most of the croissant will end up in flakes on your lap.

C. French press coffee and a bowl of oatmeal with fresh berries. You didn't microwave the oatmeal, nor did you make it in a pot that you'll leave unwashed in the sink, resulting in a permanent coating of heated milk gluing itself to the pot's surface. The oatmeal just appears on your vintage writing desk in your apartment that gets natural light, always at the perfect temperature.

3. What will your novel be about?

A. A young man attempting to discover himself through sex and vinyl records and literature he picks up at secondhand stores. The reader never learns his name. The book will be written without any punctuation and you expect it to be nominated for several prestigious awards even though no one will ever want to read through the entire thing.

B. A coming-of-age young adult novel about a girl, funnier and more ornery than you, taking a trip through Europe just like you took a trip through Europe. People will describe it as a romp. It will sell fine.

C. A marriage falling apart, a girl unearthing an age-old secret in her town, and a mute priest. Their stories intersect in a way no one ever would expect. The novel is 600 pages and critics will rave about the sparkling prose and call you a rising literary superstar.

4. What do you wear on, say, a random Tuesday?

A. Torn black jeans that you haven't gotten around to repairing, the T-shirt you slept in, and a leather jacket.

B. The same leggings you've worn all week, a bra you haven't washed in months, a black tank top, and the same sweater you've had since middle school.

C. Dark jeans, a crisp white button-down, big sunglasses, and red lipstick. You always look like an off-duty model or an on-duty Parisian.

5. How do you write?

A. In a Moleskine notebook with an expensive fountain pen. Writing is all about the aesthetics; you are a serious writer and you want everybody in your MFA program to know it.

B. Rarely, and on a laptop with keys stained with Chinese food splatter and a screen with a dead black space that runs a full inch down the right side that's been there since you dropped the computer while standing up to answer the door for the Chinese food deliveryman.

C. On a vintage typewriter that you got as a gift from a very famous writer that you'll decline to name, because you're not that type of person. You whip through pages with ease—you are the type of person for whom a typewriter makes sense and not the type of person who would spend $450 on a typewriter that will gather dust on the shelf by your bed because the opportunity never feels quite right to actually sit down and use it. The typewriter always feels right for you. The morning light comes through your window, and your desk has flowers that you never forget to water. Oh, it's not easy, of course not. Writing is a craft, and when you're done with the first draft, you have the patience and fortitude to sit down with your red pen and edit until the prose is as dazzling as you are.

If you answered mostly As

You are *that guy* in your MFA program. Not necessarily a guy, but just, you know: that guy. The one who wears the slouchy beanie for the carefully cultivated effect of nonchalant artist, the one who always talks in class, who writes pretentious poetry and says he's working on a novel that no one's ever seen. There are two options for your future: (1) You will give up as a writer after a single rejection from the *New Yorker* or (2) you write a slim, experimental novel that becomes a surprise runaway bestseller and you will float through New York for the rest of your career, guest editing anthologies and fucking nineteen-year-olds in your East Village apartment.

If you answered mostly Bs

You will get a job writing—first for a magazine and then for the same magazine's website when the magazine is no longer in print. You will become the type of person who spends more and more time online, scrolling through social media and allowing your brain's once-sharp edges to gradually become round. When you do write a book, you will wonder if it was for the right reasons. You care too much what other people think.

If you answered mostly Cs

You are a liar. You exist only in the fantasies of someone who answered mostly Bs, especially after she eats a heavy lunch and succumbs to two doughnuts that someone left in the office kitchenette and feels her stomach pressing up against her waistband. Someone who answered mostly Cs would have always been in control. She would have a defined jawline, and green eyes, and wouldn't contemplate getting a nose job because her nose would already be perfect. She would be described as willowy. She would write every day and be praised constantly even though she wouldn't need it because she doesn't base her self-esteem on external praise.

There is a folk legend every student knows but that no one has ever been told, a legend that has traveled across the globe and through the generations like a deadly airborne virus, or that way you all knew how to draw that cartoon *S* on your notebook paper, starting with six vertical lines in two rows. The legend is as follows: If a professor is more than fifteen minutes late to class, the class is canceled, and every student is permitted to go home.

It is tested only one time in your entire tenure as a student: the first day of Introduction to Fiction Writing.

The class is a workshop, only fifteen people, and tucked

into a corner room on the second floor of the library. With the library's concrete walls (another neo-brutalist addition to the campus sometime in the 1970s) and densely packed shelves, it has the eerie gloom that seems like it's always sundown. You had a certain idea of what an Ivy League university library would look like—Raphaelesque paintings on the walls; mahogany desks, each with its own cozy green banker's lamp; walls of books dappled by sunlight and reachable only by ladder. This is a barren structure, built in the '60s and close to the ground. Most of the books are kept in subterranean basement stacks, with automatic lights so finicky and difficult to activate that you've found yourself using the flashlight on your phone to find the tome you want.

This classroom hasn't been set up for a writing workshop: all of the desks face different directions, so you all sit facing different directions. But heads are all turned toward the clock. Your professor is now officially sixteen minutes late. You look at one another.

"This is A204, right?" someone asks.

You all murmur your assent.

"Level two fiction writing?" someone else asks.

"Wait, no. Arabic, right?"

There are more mumbles, and it is established that the rest of you are there for level two fiction, not Arabic. "Oh. Oh, shit," the Arabic-taker says, and he heaves his backpack up and leaves the room. You hear his footsteps echo down the hallway, past the stacks and all the way to the library's central spiraling staircase, but it's the only set of footsteps you hear. No one is coming from the other direction.

Seventeen minutes after two.

"It's the first day," one boy suggests to no one in particular. He already has the two course books out of his bag and stacked neatly on his desk. "Maybe he's just finding his way."

And then, like he's been summoned, the door opens and a man who can only be the professor enters. His age is impossible to determine: He could be a fifty-five-year-old with a good, even tan and a thick head of black hair, or a thirty-year-old with a world-weary expression. He isn't smiling when he enters, and he traces over every one of you with his gray eyes before settling at the desk in the front of the room. He looks more like someone who would play a young, troublemaking uncle on *The O.C.* than a professor.

"I was trying to get the registrar to change rooms. Hate these back-of-the-library rooms," he says. No one responds. "Come on, gather your chairs around. Just...circle up."

You do. None of you have seen this professor before or heard any stories about him from upperclassmen. He is a visiting professor, you're pretty sure. There is no mythology attached to him.

"So I'm going to be your professor this semester," he says, smirking to reveal perfectly straight teeth. You hadn't known people smirked outside of romance novels before this. "I figured since it's the first day you might as well just ask me any questions you might have about me."

None of you have ever begun a college class with the professor asking for an interview.

The boy with his books out asks the first question like a cautious step onto a frozen lake.

So, where are you from?

—Florida.

Where were you before this?

—Teaching in Florida.

How is this class going to be graded?

—Just...do your work. Do the reading. We'll workshop three student pieces a week.

What kind of writing do you do, mainly?

—I write books.

What kind of books do you write? you ask.

—That's a pointless question.

—Double-spaced, twelve-point font.

—Yes, this class is mandatory pass/fail.

—Ready? All right, let's open the yellow book to page 131 and talk about Tobias Wolff.

It's only as you're walking back to your dorm room that you realize the professor never actually said his name.

You look him up later with your laptop balanced on your belly and find his profile on a Florida university website: a much younger picture of him, handsome and squinting into the sun, with a brief biography noting his two books, both no doubt celebrated among a certain circle of the literati at least for a brief moment. Their descriptions are almost parodies of their genre: neither poetry nor prose, neither fiction nor memoir— *these are autobiographies of objects, manifestos of emotion, notebooks of erotica, handmade ceramic bowls of feelings. They transcend linear structure, the literary establishment, and the physical act of reading itself.* You hate them immediately.

And yet you admit to yourself, you desperately want this professor to like you. You want him to feel as though you and he are colleagues, on the same level. You, a vivacious, single-eyebrow-raising co-ed, precocious literary talent, and he the cynical, brilliant professor who sees something special in you.

Because here's the thing you can admit to yourself: You're a good writer. Sometimes even a very good writer. It's the one consistent thing about your identity that's existed from first grade on, the way you're able to sit down with a notebook and write something weird and fast and memorable.

When you were eight, you wrote a book of rhyming poems about animals at the zoo.

You were planning on illustrating each page, but the poetry-writing came faster and easier to you than the drawing. Someone would look at your drawings and know immediately you were a child; if your typed and printed words were good enough, they could be from anyone.

Come to the zoo and see the giraffe
The long-necker
Tree-wrecker
Star-checker
Giraffe.

"Mom, who is the publisher who does the Dr. Seuss books?" you asked one day while your mom was preparing turkey sandwiches for the next day.

"I...don't know," she replied.

Undeterred, you marched upstairs and found a Seuss book in your closet and identified the strange words in the bottom corner of its cover: RANDOM HOUSE.

You asked your father for a big envelope from work and

addressed it carefully with an address you found during your thirty minutes of computer time, and slid the pages inside. "Can you mail this tomorrow?" you asked your dad. He agreed.

You would be a kid-genius, a celebrant of the literary world. You were trapped in the comfortable bubble of the suburbs, on the conveyer belt of high school, college, boring job, boring marriage—then having kids and watching the whole cycle repeat itself again but this time from the opposite side. But your writing can get you out. People will *read* your writing. You will make boatloads of money and live in New York when you're not traveling the world to meet adoring fans. You will be like Dr. Seuss, read for generations, your life the fodder for endless elementary school oral reports. Your writing just has to be good enough—and maybe it is.

You have two fantasies about the professor that reappear equally frequently. The first is his fucking you, over his desk. That one creeps through your ear and into your brain at 11:30 p.m. when you're alone in your dorm room with the covers drawn up to your chin and one hand tracing the elastic band of your underwear and the red indent it made in your belly. The second fantasy is the two of you locked in a close discussion, staying for hours after class in this back room of the library after the rest of the students have gone, those peons whose analysis of Katherine Mansfield was almost comical in its simplicity compared to the commentary you were able to contribute in class, even though you only skimmed the assignment. The two of you would talk about literature and writing until the red sun sank behind the eighteenth-century wood houses that line the edges of

Brown's campus like soldiers, and then you would keep talking, in a bar, in his room, while he fucked you over his desk,
and so on.

A semester goes by with you attempting to impress him
with oblique references to Twitter followers and the fact that
you're looking for an *agent*, and did he know you almost
have an agent? "Oh, Professor, quick question. When I'm
looking for an *agent*, what really should I be looking for?"

"I wouldn't really know," he says, and slinks from the
room after the class ends, at 5:01 p.m.

Finally, you have your semester meeting with him, in
which every student is required to sign up for a fifteen-
minute slot in his office to discuss your final writing project.
You wrote a maudlin, meandering piece about a teenage girl
going to her cousin's funeral and stealing from her dead
cousin's bedroom. Nearly every other student in the class
wrote some Jack Kerouac–wannabe bullshit about a man
who is dissatisfied with his married life and wonders if ho
should just get on a train and leave it all behind. (In half
the stories, he did get on the train, and in the other half he
didn't. In one story, he jumps in front of it.) You want praise
for your voice-y first-person, unpretentious story. A beginning, a middle, and an end. No loyalty to the up-its-own-ass
literary establishment.

"Some parts of it worked," the professor says to you,
handing over the printed pages with a few nondescript red
squiggles. "Needed a more human angle. It was okay,
though."

The professor's office doesn't seem fully occupied yet,
like the condo of a newly divorced dad. He shares it with
another visiting professor, but both desks are disconcert-

ingly empty of papers or memorabilia. Only a few books with titles you don't recognize take up the empty chair beside you, and his coat is on the back of his chair. Other than that, he could disappear and no one would ever know he worked here.

"What does that mean?" you ask, the word *okay* expanding like a balloon in your brain and pushing everything else out. *Okay. Just okay. Okay, but not great. Mediocre. Okay. Okay?* "I mean, what specifically could I improve?"

"The part in the cousin's bedroom was good. I want more exploration of that sort of emotional conflict."

But his words might as well be the buzzing trombone of an adult in a Peanuts cartoon. He didn't say it was good. He didn't say you were a good writer. He was acting like you were just one more of the faceless and uninspired students he is burdened to teach between his own bouts of genius. He doesn't care about you or your work at all.

"But...but I'm writing a book," you sputter. "I'm trying to write a young adult book, and it's going to have a similar voice to this story. I mean..." And what else do you have to lose? It's the end of the semester and he's given you nothing, not even the indication that he gives a shit about teaching this class. "Am I good enough?"

"Look," the professor says. His tan has faded a bit after six months in Providence and not Florida. His hair has gone gray around the temples, but unfortunately the effect is still "distinguished literary intellectual" and not "mediocre middle-aged man." "I think," and he hisses a bit, sucking air through his teeth, "you are probably going to be a very successful *commercial* writer."

The word *commercial* now reverberates through the small

office overrun with papers. He says it like a shameful truth, like he hates to have to be the one to tell you this, but them's the facts. Sorry, kid, I just call 'em like I see it.

"Thanks," you say. *And fuck you*, you think.

Continue reading.

WHICH *LORD OF THE RINGS* CHARACTER ARE YOU, BASED ON YOUR EATING DISORDER?

"You say you don't want to be losing any more weight," the therapist said, tsking and *ratatat*ing at the clipboard in her hands with a pencil. The pencil was inscribed with her own name and office number. "And yet you're down four pounds since last week."

"Last week it was also colder outside," you say. "I was wearing a sweater, I think."

The therapist just gives you that "I'm not sad, I'm just disappointed" look, as you shuffle back into your Birkenstocks and return to your perch on her couch, across from her chair.

"Why do you think you're losing weight, Dana?" the therapist asks in her calm, even therapist voice. You wish she wouldn't use the therapist voice. You're pretty sure she isn't even a therapist; the plaque on her door actually says DIETICIAN. NUTRITIONIST. CONSULTANT. And yet here she is, with a waiting room filled with anorexic teenagers and back issues of *O Magazine* and a couch with a box of tissues next to it. You and your mom just call her by her first name, Lisa, as in, "Did you make another appointment to see Lisa next week?" The answer is always yes. Going to Lisa is part of your defensive strategy that allows temporary reprieve from your mother's constant monitoring, which she calls concern.

Here is the game you and Lisa play every week:

She weighs you.

She says you've lost weight.

You feel guilty—the slightest bit relieved, but mostly guilty. It would make the rest of the hour go by so much easier if you had just held in your pee this morning before you came and drank a full glass of water and ate a bigger-than-usual bowl of oatmeal. But since you've lost weight, and Lisa's job is to make sure you don't lose any more weight, you now have the pleasure of spending upward of forty minutes smiling and pretending to take notes as Lisa makes insane suggestions: "How about add another slice of cheese to your sandwich at lunch?" "A milkshake is a good dessert to increase calories!" "Have you considered eating a mid-morning snack?"

Thank you, Lisa, for your brilliant insight. Please, could you repeat that last one so I could write it down? *Miiid-mooooorning snack.* Maybe yogurt, you say? Got it. Wow. Brilliant. Life-changing. You're a miracle worker.

Yes, yes, yes, yes. Agree to everything, change nothing, come back next week and repeat it all over.

There's another strategy you try sometimes, the one you'll try today when it feels like agreeing one more time to "using whole milk in your coffee instead of skim!" will cause your organs to crawl out through your mouth and strangle you: You'll be honest.

"Look," you say. "I'm not actually, medically, underweight."

She agrees. You have about ten pounds left before a doctor might formally rebuke your BMI as worrisome, and ten more beyond that before a stranger on the street might think you look *sick* instead of just a pretty, teenage size 2.

"But," Lisa counters in a well-practiced tone—her attempt to sound halfway between Mary Poppins and Mr. Rogers, "we're less concerned with your weight and more concerned with your *thought process* surrounding it. You've become paranoid about your weight and restrictive in your eating in a way that doesn't reflect the truth of the real world."

"Okay, but doesn't it, though?" You know you're not going to be productive; there is no endgame in which the therapist declares *You win!* and sends you home with a signed certificate that says *GIRL ALLOWED TO EAT HOWEVER SHE WANTS NO MATTER WHAT BECAUSE SHE'S SO SMART* but now that you've started, you can't stop. "The truth of the real world is that it sucks to be overweight. Especially when you're an overweight girl. Being thin is like the most boring superpower in the world: Villains cower in fear from Everything-Goes-A-Little-Bit-Easier-For-Her Girl! Clothes fall correctly on her! Boys pay attention to her! Strangers don't give her weird looks! Yowza! Pow! (Useless as her powers are for fighting crime, they'd still probably let Everything-Goes-A-Little-Bit-Easier-For-Her Girl join the Avengers. I mean, they let bow-and-arrow guy join the Avengers.)

"It sucks, yes. It's the actual worst that this double standard exists, but it does. Everyone on this planet is biased in favor of skinny people. We think they're smarter and prettier and more competent. And as a young person trying to succeed, I want people to think those things about me. So, no, I don't think me trying to be skinny is something that 'doesn't reflect the truth of the real world.'"

Lisa twirls the pencil in her hand, but she doesn't pause before she responds. "You're a feminist, Dana. Surely you know that a woman's weight doesn't reflect anything about her."

"Of course I know that," you fire back. "It's just everyone else that doesn't know that. So if given the choice, I'd rather count calories and be skinny and reap all of those unfair advantages. It's like a cost–benefit thing. Yes, counting calories all the time is annoying, but it's an overall better way to be compared to how the world treats being a fat girl."

"You know," Lisa continued, as if she had planned her response before you had even said a word. "You can have a good figure without obsessing over calories. Eating intuitively, for example. I promise, if you bring your weight up just five pounds, your brain chemistry will return to a state where you aren't always obsessing about what you eat."

Thin People always say shit like that. "Eating intuitively," is Thin Person garbage, just like "I'm addicted to exercise!" and "This is just too sweet for me. I couldn't possibly finish it." You, by contrast, are a Fat Person who just happens to be thin at the moment, and your body is fighting at every opportunity to return, like entropy, to its natural resting state. If you tried to "eat intuitively," nothing would stop you from having a bag of chips at lunch. And then a cookie. And then a second cookie. And then cupcakes for someone's birthday. Before you knew it, there would be nothing keeping your calories in check at all. Within a week, it would be The Purge and you'd be wearing a pig mask and threatening people with a baseball bat for a couple of Mallomars.

But you can't explain any of that to a Thin Person.

"Yeah," you say. "Okay. Maybe you're right. What were you saying about whole milk again?" It's useless. You spend the rest of the hour taking inane notes and nodding and half-smiling with an expression you designed as "rueful, resistant teen finally opening up to the light."

Lisa is just doing her job, but so are you. You are doing the job of a girl who wants to be successful in the real world. The counting calories, the lying in bed and pressing your palm against your hip bones to make sure they jut out far enough, the way you yank at your jeans until they're baggy enough to fit a full fist in the waistband—they're just the price of admission. You're doing as you're told. You're living as a human woman in all her exquisite misery, exactly the way you've been taught.

Back when you were a sophomore in high school, you read in a magazine (one with *Women's* cheerfully in its name, a B-list celebrity on the cover with a swatch of glowing abs emerging from a pair of Lycra booty shorts) the number of calories a woman should eat to maintain her weight. The answer is a clean, even 1,800 calories. The number itself is ripe like a fruit—two full zeros at the end, the eight pinched in the middle like a perfect hourglass figure. The magazine advises 300 calories for breakfast, 400 calories for lunch, and 500 calories for dinner, with one 200-calorie snack and one 200-calorie dessert. It's that easy. If you obey those rules, you will be a normal, thin woman. Any calories you eat over that amount will be stored, like wheat in a silo, to create lumps of bulging fat and unhappiness in your life.

You become obsessed with the terror of pulling on a particular pair of jeans; these pants force you to pull the fabric tight across your stomach to coerce them into buttoning. You see the red marks left beneath your belly button at the end of the day and knead at them, half lovingly, half loathingly. You are five foot six in a Jewish community and you were tall fast: taller than your mom, taller than your older sister, taller than most of your friends by at least several inches. It makes you feel big, like a lumbering oaf escorting your petite friends, brought along as a mission of goodwill between the pixie fairy and the ogre communities. You are never the ingénue. You are smart and you are loud about it, raising your hand every question and debating anything, anywhere, with anyone who would make the mistake of engaging you. You imagine your manner with boys to be the flirty, aggressive banter of a romantic comedy heroine; you don't yet realize playful repartee doesn't work on suburban teenage boys, especially if you don't look like Kate Hudson.

In third grade, you and your friend sat in the hallway outside your classroom. Your friend planted her feet in front of her and pulled her knees to her chest, showing you how even when she presses her knees tight together, her kneecaps always hit before the dangling flesh below could touch. You tried it. The flesh of your thighs flowed together and closed the space between your legs. Your friend looked over at you pityingly. "Strange," she said before turning back to her own still-bony child's legs.

And so you read a magazine telling you that you're supposed to eat 1,800 calories a day to maintain your weight. You hadn't been counting calories before. You might have been eating double that, triple that for all you know. That must be why your jeans have been tightening, why you see photographs of yourself and fixate on the size of your arm and whether or not there's any flab visible. You hadn't been counting your calories the way a thin, responsible chic woman should, the type of woman who wears all black and high heels and hails a taxi to chauffeur her to a high-powered job in New York City (most of your visions of what a successful woman looked like came from *13 Going on 30* and *The Devil Wears Prada*). You repeat those numbers like a mantra, and they infect your brain. You want to be smaller, so what do you do?

What do you do?

A. You think back to something from years ago, how in the back of your middle school library, you had come across a book that was more Lifetime movie than novel. It was about the perils of eating disorders and how easily this poor, cherubic suburban teenager became seduced by the demon that is bulimia when the popular girl in her class showed her the secret of putting a finger down her throat and canceling out the food before she digested it. The book was meant to scare the reader because of the horror and the shame, how even though the main character got skinny, it wasn't worth it because she took it too far and had to deal with Consequences. You wouldn't take it too far. You just don't want your jeans to be too tight.

Turn to page 40.

B. You Google images of models with bony thighs and arms like baby birds. They don't pine over boys who gradually stop returning their instant messages or who only want to be friends with them. They don't deal with awkward silences. If you lost weight, you could be one of them. And the faster you lose the weight, the faster your life would improve. You Google "how to lose ten pounds fast." Then "how to lose ten pounds in a week." There are people out there with the self-control and willpower to be skinny. They're not better than you. You count the calories of everything you eat. You trap yourself within 1,800. If you don't go over 1,800, you won't gain weight. All you need to do from there is eat just a little bit less.

Turn to page 61.

IT BEGAN AS A LOW MURMUR FROM DOWN THE HALL: a door opening, multiple pairs of feet climbing stairs, giggles, the hushing of giggles. You were ostensibly in your pajamas, but you were still wearing a bra and cover-up. Too much makeup would have jinxed it—no, just a little bit of cover-up so if midnight came and went without you getting tapped for an a cappella group, you wouldn't have to go through the tragic exercise of wiping away mascara gutters.

But, you admit to yourself, allowing your stomach to somersault into your throat, you definitely hear *something*, in the hallway, definitely something. When you audition for college a cappella—going from room to room in the engineering building on a Thursday night, singing the same sixteen measures for each group, one at a time—you present them all with an index card featuring your name, voice range, and dorm room. The dorm room is so tonight, if you've been selected (and drafted through the proper procedures at the rigorous, highly secret, and invariably drunk meeting of the intergalactic council of a cappella), your new family will kidnap you at midnight. Those unlucky unselected wait by their windows all night like stood-up prom dates.

The murmur becomes louder. And then, it's a vigorous knocking on your door. "I'll get it," you shout to your roommate, leaping off your bed. Your roommate is in a bathrobe and fuzzy pink slippers like a 1950s housewife. She just looks at you.

You fling the door open, and then you are suddenly face-to-face with every member of the Alef Beats, Brown University's premiere Jewish-themed a cappella group.

"You're in the Bee-aaaats, and it feels so good!" they sing to the tune of The Lonely Island's "I've Just Had Sex," mouths gleefully wide, stomping and clapping until every door in the hallway has opened to reveal a peering face. "You're in the Beeaaaaaats, and you'll never go baaa-ack, to the not-in-the-Beats way of the past!"

It feels a bit like a roomful of people singing "Happy Birthday" to you; you aren't sure whether to sing along, or clap, or smile, and so you do a little bit of all of that. They fling Hershey's Kisses and confetti into your room. A beat-boxer, the heartthrob of the Jewish a cappella group, leans against the doorway and winks. "Grab your shoes!" someone shouts, and you retreat to your room to gather whatever basic necessities (phone? keys? money? will you need money?) are in easy grasp.

"I hope you're going to come back to clean this up," your roommate says, eyeing a single chocolate Kiss that dared to roll to her side of the room.

"I will, I will!" you call over your shoulder, and you join the romping, frolicking horde, down the steps of the dorm and out into the night.

The destination, you discover, is Jen's house. You do not yet know who Jen is, nor where her house is, but that doesn't matter when it's midnight and you're in college and you're running across Lincoln Field singing a song about just having had sex (the flask that was passed around somehow helped the lyrics revert back to their original form). You learn a flurry of names in the dark: Ben, Korama, Alex, Anna, Ben G, Rachel, Sydney, Sofaya, and Jen—your host for an evening of bagels and Manischewitz, appropriate for your Jewish theme.

"I swear," Rachel says, "my friends thought I was in an a cappella group called the Olive Beats for a full year."

"That's how you know who's not Jewish," one of the boys, maybe Ben, says.

"*I'm* not Jewish!" Rachel calls back.

Korama turns to you with a gaze of maternal benevolence, doing her duty to help the Baby Beats—as those who were inducted that night would be known for the next full year. "We're like, half Jewish as a group, *maybe*."

"I'm half Jewish!" another girl, maybe Susan? offers.

"Yeah," Korama says. "Like, half. We're Jew-ish."

You've made it to Jen's off-campus place—an old Providence town house with wooden shutters and a big porch. Jen opens the creaking door and ushers the group into the kitchen. Korama grabs a bagel and then continues. "That means, like, we sing things if they have a tenuous Jewish connection. Like Maroon 5 counts. And obviously Yael Naim. But also, literally, whatever we want."

You sit gingerly on the strange couch. "So being the Jewish a cappella group means...?"

"Jewish-themed," Korama corrects. "Jewish-themed a cappella group. And it basically means we sing at high holiday services and drink Manischewitz. Speaking of which!"

Someone—one of the boys—thrusts a paper cup filled with purple wine into your hand. "Oh, no thank you," you say. "I don't really drink. I mean, I have an early class tomorrow."

You don't. But it's easier than explaining that you've eaten all of your calories for the day. Besides, if you avoid drinking as a rule, you'll probably prevent the freshman fifteen. Alcohol is all sugar anyway. It's not like drinking is *good* for you.

But it's been hours since dinner in the cafeteria (salad with vinegar, grilled chicken breast, two sweet potato medallions) and as you watch the rest of the group tear into the bagel bag, smearing their selection with cream cheese off plastic knives, you wish you could too. But a bagel is the carb equivalent of *at least* five slices of bread, a voice with an unknown source chastises you. If you were to eat a bagel now, everything you've done to be skinny, everything you've sacrificed, would be for nothing.

You have to leave before they realize you're not eating or drinking anything. You can't be that weird, restrictive-eating girl with a group of people you just met, who *chose* you and came to your dorm to sing to you in front of thirty other freshmen.

"I think I have to head out," you say. "That early class."

"Awwwww," someone says.

"See you at rehearsal," Ben says.

"BEATS FOR LIFE!" the other Ben says. He says *life* with two syllables. Ly-uff.

And so, you slink out onto the street, the first to leave the party, and speed-walk across the inky-wet grass until you're back in your own room. Your roommate is asleep, complete with noise-canceling headphones and a *Breakfast at Tiffany's*–style eye mask. You turn on your lamp and sit at your desk, too wired to sleep.

You are hungry, you admit to yourself. And that chicken breast for dinner was small, probably just 60 calories and not the 100 you mentally accounted for. And you did only have those two slices of sweet potato, not an entire sweet potato (you had counted them as a whole one just to be safe). You could eat something else. Something small.

So, with the deliberation of a neurosurgeon, you reach under your bed, into the plastic Container Store bin that your mother packed full of healthy dorm-room snacks, and unwrap a Kashi Honey Almond Flax bar (140 calories).

You stare at the yellow oat flakes and artificially glistening almond pieces. You usually don't eat after ten as a rule because you read somewhere that those calories become belly fat.

Fuck it. You eat the oat bar and it tastes more delicious than anything you can remember eating ever before. Your chewing becomes mechanical. Maybe this is your first orgasm.

Still chewing its final bite, you unwrap a second Kashi Honey Almond Flax bar and while you're making the decision of whether or not you should eat it, it's already gone and you're throwing away both wrappers in the trash, burying them deep so you won't have to look at them.

There are only two bars left in the box. As soon as they're gone, you won't be tempted anymore. And so, for the greater good, you finish the two last bars and bury them with their brethren. You're full but it doesn't hurt yet. You don't feel the sides of your stomach pressing up against you from the inside. You've been hungry for so long, and now you want to be full. What's the worst that could happen? You're only a few hundred calories over your limit for the day. Maybe you'll gain a fraction of a pound. Even if the worst happened, if you gained a pound, it would be fine. You grant yourself permission to gain one pound. You got picked for an a cappella group. You deserve to celebrate.

What else is in your room? Three-quarters of a box of Kashi GOLEAN cereal, sawdusty rabbit food they describe as "protein twigs." Back home you used to pour three times the quarter cup for a breakfast with only 9 grams of sugar.

(Years later, you still remember that number. You could be using that brain space to remember names, places, lines of poetry. Instead, you remember how much sugar was in a portion of cereal. Sherlock Holmes would be ashamed of your use of attic space.) You had been scared, coming to college, and a little panicked, because you weren't going to have constant use of a measuring cup to protect yourself from too much cereal. Your mom had known, when she saw you fingering the plastic measuring cups at Bed Bath & Beyond. "Dana. Honey," she said with such sadness in her voice. "Don't be that person at college."

Well, no measuring cup now. You pour a mound into the Plexiglas bowl you also use to microwave 100-calorie packets of oatmeal with water. You slosh almond milk on top of the mountain of cereal until it floats, far more than the half-cup estimate you usually limit yourself to, and you inhale the bowl's contents in the semidarkness of your room, not listening to music or watching television, just focusing on getting the food inside your body quickly, before your brain could change its mind. You drink the remaining almond milk from the bowl and pour another mound of cereal to drown in yet more almond milk. Only a quarter of a box left now. As soon as it's gone, you won't be tempted anymore.

Next, a powdery packet of oatmeal you heat in the microwave without even rinsing the bowl first. You squeeze in two sticks of honey your mom sent you in your Rosh Hashanah package back in the fall. You hadn't touched them until now—too much sugar. You squeeze the rest of the honey sticks directly into your mouth, gnawing at the crystalized corners with your teeth. As soon as they're gone, you won't be tempted anymore.

By the time you've finished three bowls of oatmeal, your brain begins to acknowledge the ache in your stomach. It hurts to move. You aren't sure whether you're imagining it or whether you've actually eaten enough for the stuff to have filled your stomach completely and begun piling on top of itself and crawling up your gullet. You feel like a goose being fattened for foie gras, and yet you are so, so close to drowning the knot of anxiety in your stomach.

You try to count the calories of your feast but give up when you hit 2,000. You've put on at least a pound, but that's okay; you could gain a pound. When you drag yourself to the clean cell of the shared one-person bathroom in the hallway, then try to stick your finger down your throat, it's not because you're scared to gain that tiny increment of weight; no, it's just your stomach feels so uncomfortable. You don't want to feel like this anymore. You want a clean start, for the contents of your stomach to disappear from your stomach and deposit themselves neatly into a toilet where they can be swept away down pipes and you can forget all about this and never let it happen again.

Does it happen again?

A. No. It doesn't. You can stop yourself. You have better self-control than this, don't you? You had the willpower to count calories for two years straight, and now you're going to let some Kashi get the best of you? Kashi tastes like wet cardboard. You know it, they know it, everyone knows it. It's wet cardboard that women eat to punish themselves like that albino monk self-flagellating in *The Da Vinci Code*. You ate all of the Kashi in your room and now your punishment is complete. Time to get back to normal.

Turn to page 53.

B. Yes. Again and again, eating until you can't move and then throwing it up becomes less of a habit and more of a hobby, something you look forward to like reruns of a favorite television show. It fills the time. It will make you skinny. It will make you feel better.

Continue reading.

It was so easy in that kids' book about bulimia, that preteen specter of what was to come for you, the Ghost of Self-Sabotage Future. In the book's second chapter, the chubby protagonist with frizzy brown hair walked in on the most popular girl in school retching her guts out in the girls' bathroom at lunch. "It's easy," the popular girl said, waggling her first two fingers (fingers are always waggling in these types of scenarios). The frizzy-haired protagonist held up a finger before her like Horatio's skull and made the fateful decision to insert it into her gullet, emptying herself of everything she'd eaten that day and sealing her deal with the devil to get skinny.

It is not easy for you.

You shove two fingers into your mouth until your front teeth graze your last knuckle. You waggle like your life depends on it, all the while mentally counting down the imaginary one-hour deadline you remember reading about somewhere until calories are absorbed.

All you need to do is trigger a gag reflex and then all of this will be over: the sweating, the nausea, the kneeling in a freshman dorm bathroom stall, the fear that someone will hear what you're doing. Just trigger a gag reflex.

It doesn't work. You spit in the toilet and wash your hands and then crawl back into your bed, where you click mindlessly through the Internet until it's dark outside your window.

Before you try again, you read tips on websites with warning labels at the top, and study excerpts from books about people who overcame eating disorders like they were how-to manuals. Most of the tricks don't work for you, but some of them do—tricks that you won't write here because however interesting the particular details of your misery might be, it's far outweighed by the certainty that someone would want to try them.

Here is what happens when you finally manage to make yourself throw up: shaking as if you have a fever; sweating so much your shirt sticks to your back and your hair turns freezing cold along your scalp; the acidy sour taste of vomit living in your throat and under your tongue and on your toothbrush; feeling the icy splash of toilet water on your face when you manage to get something out.

Here is what they never told you in those pretty finger-wagging books: It never all comes up, and it doesn't come up like the vomit you're used to, the salmon-colored mush of stomach flu or airport sushi. This comes up in bready lumps like the pictures of aborted fetuses they put on billboards when you drive an hour outside a big city. These are pieces that were never meant to come up the other way.

You imagine the scene like the black-and-white introduction of a TV infomercial: you on your knees, gagging and clenching, hair wet with sweat and toilet water turning straight to the camera and breaking the fourth wall: "There's got to be a better way!" You try cutting your feast with massive quantities of Diet Coke by the strange logic that the carbonation might levitate mush out of your belly when you gag like it's Wonka's Fizzy Lifting Drink. You Google *syrup of ipecac*. You check the CVS on the corner. They don't have it. You call the CVS in town.

"Excuse me," you say. You're already walking toward the store. It's a twenty-minute walk but there's nothing more important to do today than get yourself clean of everything you ate. "Do you have syrup of ipecac?"

The CVS employee sounds confused when she says, "I don't think so. What do you need that for?"

"My dog," you say. "I need to make my dog throw up. She ate chocolate."

"No," the woman on the other end of the phone says with pity and derision in her voice. "No, we definitely don't sell that here."

You'd read one magazine piece about a celebrity who made it through the other side of bulimia to share her misery porn with the *People* magazine–reading public. She said that she would start all of her binges with a "marker food," something fluorescent-colored, vivid enough so that when she finally saw streaks of orange Cheetos dust or blood-red sugar-free Jell-O, she'd know she'd vomited the entire binge up, reached the final stratum layer of compounded carbohydrates like an archaeologist excavating deeper and deeper into the earth.

Back when this all started, when you felt ambitious, you'd

begin by eating a family-sized bag of nacho Doritos, but you could never, ever make yourself vomit enough to see the streaks of orange chemicals. One more retch, you would bargain with yourself. One more, and that'll be enough. You thought vomiting would leave you cleansed—a shortcut to Gwyneth Paltrow-dom for those without willpower. Instead, you're left nauseous and shaking on an unwashed bathroom floor, fantasizing about someone rescuing you but also terrified that someone will find you.

You retreat back to your dorm room. At first, you were fastidious about cleaning the oatmeal-colored crust from beneath the semiprivate dorm toilet, paranoid that the next occupant would hear your retching, watch you exit, and then see your mess, but now you've stopped caring. Let someone confront you. What will another eighteen-year-old college freshman say to the girl down the hall that they barely know?

Now that you've vomited whatever you could, you can finish the haul of junk food you purchased from CVS, floating, manic, down the aisles, not making eye contact with anyone. Now you can go to the dining hall and drink bowlfuls of cereal from your lonely perch in the corner behind your laptop, hoping that the cafeteria staff won't notice how many bowls you're going through.

You haven't lost weight yet. You've gained almost twenty pounds, and now you're struggling to remember which pair of jeans in your closet fit and you avoid taking pictures so you can pretend you look like you do in your memory: your senior year of high school, when you were all elbows and teeth. You can't stop eating—now that you've tasted non-baked potato chips and non-skinny ice cream, you can't go

back; you can't stop yourself on lonely Friday nights when
you need something to do with your hands and your mouth
while you watch YouTube videos of stand-up comedy routines you've seen a hundred times before. And if you're
going to eat it, you're going to have to throw it up. You're
trapped, but it's only for now, because this time is the last
time, you promise.

It's 4:00 p.m. on a Tuesday night, and you have no assign-
ments due tomorrow, no reading you want to do, no friends
you want to see, no parties to go to tonight. You are sitting
on your dorm room bed, bored of scrolling through dozens of
reddit pages but there's nothing else to do. You need a hit of
dopamine, of attention, of something to contain the boredom
that gnaws at you like rats.

How do you self-soothe?

A. Twitter. Let the endless scroll of meaningless content lull
   you into a stupor. Post a joke and hit notifications again
   and again to refresh, trying to get another rush of
   dopamine from the people hitting "like" and "retweet"
   on your observation that technically, it's only ONE Star
   WAR, singular.

Turn to page 55.

B. Food. Get another thin black plastic bag full of processed
   calories, let your eyes go glassy, and rewatch *Gilmore
   Girls* on Netflix while you devour it all in twenty-five
   minutes flat. Then you can pass out, wrappers shamefully tucked away in the black bag and pushed to the

bottom of your trash can, as if you're a child who hasn't yet developed object permanence: If you can't see the evidence, it never happened.

Turn to page 61.

THERE'S NO RECOVERY. Of course there isn't. This isn't a chipper first-person sob story as told to a writer for a women's magazine under the guise of female empowerment. You are trapped and trapped for life because you are a woman in the world in 2018 and your brain is already wired against you, polluted with expectations and temptations and dozens of versions of yourself following you like ghosts, dragging you into immobility: Are you the salad girl who cares about wholeness and wellness, who Instagrams green smoothies and glistening acai bowls? Are you the girl who gets skinny drinking only black coffee? Are you the girl who chows down burgers on dates and beers because you're cool and always game? Or the relatable, self-deprecating girl who shares bottles of red wine with a friend while watching *The Bachelorette* ironically and eats ice cream straight from the pint?

To you, food will always be a costume.

You will never be a Thin Person who just eats whatever she wants and works out because she just loves the feeling. The type of person who sacrifices her sandwiches for salads for a few days with a shrug if her jeans get too tight before going back to eating whatever she wants.

You will always be the girl who eats the extra slice of pizza at the party, frantically looking around for confirmation that someone is eating at least as much as you are and, if they aren't, that at least no one is noticing how much you're eating. You will weigh yourself every morning and fantasize about how much happier you'd be if you were thinner.

(*Nonsense*, a practical voice in your brain says. *But is it?* whispers another voice. After all, can we really pretend as though the world doesn't make existence infinitely easier for the skinny?)

You will live for the next eight years somewhere on a sliding scale across seventy pounds.

Here is what recovery means: You have landed somewhere in the middle. You don't throw up anymore. You allow yourself to eat most everything you want, even if you hate yourself afterward. You tell yourself to eat more fruits and vegetables. You try and fail to get into a habit of working out "just to be healthy." The best thing you can say about recovery is you think about calories less often. The math in your brain is no longer constantly ticking away like a metronome, siphoning your attention away from the rest of the world. The best thing about this recovery is that sometimes you allow yourself to forget you have a body at all. That is the best you'll get.

Turn to page 74.

THERE ISN'T ENOUGH TO DO ON THE INTERNET. It's 11:00 p.m. and you've already seen all of the Aziz Ansari stand-up specials that are freely available on YouTube. You've refreshed BuzzFeed and refreshed BuzzFeed again and scrolled so far down their site the quizzes have become non-sensical ("Which 90210 Character Are You Based on Your Favorite Kinds of Sandwich?").

Twitter would be a welcome distraction if you had more followers. You generally hover around 400, which is impressive enough for your friends, all wannabe comedians who write for the *Brown Noser* and send you endless Facebook invitations to improv shows. But at 11:00 on a Tuesday night, there just aren't enough people online for you to interact with. Your tweets get five favorites, maybe six, before they stall and drift farther down the feed and into obscurity, casualties in the Internet's endless advance for immediacy. You could write something but you have no good ideas. So, out of options and nearly comatose with boredom, it appears as though you'll just have to do your homework.

There are five stories that you're supposed to read before workshop tomorrow. You'll go over them with a blue pen you dig from the bottom of your backpack with comments like "great line here!" and "maybe add more detail?"

The first story is about a man who thinks his wife might be having an affair but isn't sure. The man is considering boarding a plane but can't remember if his ticket is re-fundable. "Maybe add more detail?" you write in the empty space after the final paragraph. "Like, so the main character feels like a human being?"

The second story is about a man who sleeps with the girl who works at the local coffee shop and then decides he doesn't want to sleep with her anymore.

The third is about a man leaving his wife and then sleeping with the girl who works at the local record store.

You realize all three stories are by boys in your class, the type who come in black T-shirts with holes at the collar and take notes in Moleskine notebooks and roll their eyes if a girl compares something to Jane Austen. They're that boy you've seen smoking outside the Rock—the main library at Brown. (There's a story they tell about it on tours for prospective students and their eager parents, how John D. Rockefeller was upset that students were calling his namesake library "the Rock"—until they started calling it "the John" instead.) Those boys are always on the stairs of the Rock, each reclining back with one foot kicked up behind him so his body is straight and flat as a board, forming the hypotenuse of a right triangle between the ground and the building.

The stories were pretentious, but their worst crime, you realized, was that they were boring. You don't care about the lonely white man who rides a train and wonders what more the country owes him. You don't care about these men who have sex with women and feel sorry for themselves because the girls (the women become girls after they've been fucked) don't understand how complicated they are. Terrible writing so often bejewels itself in the trappings of J. D. Salinger and Hemingway and Updike and Cheever and shouts, "Me too!" as it glides into any room. There is nothing profound about not deciding to name a main character. "It's meant to represent *every* man," you can imagine one of the boys explaining tomorrow, rolling his eyes behind his Warby Parkers and massaging the bridge of his nose as if he's so much better than all of this because he's convinced himself he understood *Ulysses*. No, you think, you just wrote a bad story and hid it behind a cardboard cutout of what you think a good story would look like.

You shove the stack of stapled packets off your bed and pull your laptop open again. Creating a new Twitter account is easy—all you need is a username and a new email address to register it with. You give the system your Brown.edu email this time, and where it asks you for your name, you type ThatGuyInYourWritingWorkshop. Too many characters. You get rid of the "That." GuyInYourWritingWorkshop. Still too long. GuyInYourWorkshop? But a workshop could be anything. If this is going to work, it needs to be specific. GuyInYourMFA. The next logical step to the self-aggrandizing literary genius in his own mind in an undergraduate writing workshop: graduate school. This Twitter account would be the voice of That Guy in every MFA program, the one who nitpicks and wheedles and willfully misunderstands, who believes himself to be smarter than the professor and uncompromised in his artistic principles because no one has ever asked him to sell out. He would be the type to write novels halfway between poetry and prose, published by tiny presses and praised by the three people who read them. He would be That Guy in Your MFA. And he would be you.

The first tweet erupts from your fingertips. "You should really use quotation marks, my professor said. Clearly, I replied, you aren't familiar with the work of Cormac McCarthy." You hit TWEET and begin writing another. "Perhaps add a dream sequence?" and then a third. ("When my protagonist suffocates the prostitute, he's really suffocating the American Dream") and a fourth and a fifth, and before midnight you've tweeted forty-four times.

You've gained a few dozen followers, more from luck than anything, but somehow even that number is enough to keep your phone dinging nearly continuously. *Ding. Ding. Ding. Ding, ding, di—di—di—ding.* One ding won't end before it's superseded by another. You decide to accelerate the follower count. First you post the account on Facebook, all faux-modesty ("Hey, this is a thing I made. Please follow it so I don't feel like a complete loser lol!") and then by retweeting @GuyInYourMFA on your primary account. You screenshot your forty-four tweets and upload the pictures to Tumblr, and then to reddit. You go to sleep and wake up to so many notifications on your phone that it takes five full minutes to scroll through them.

People tweet at you, calling you a genius. Your Tumblr post has 10,000 notes (you had no idea a Tumblr post could even get that many notes), and your post on reddit has 500, plus about a hundred more comments, mostly from more people also calling you a genius. You turn the dinging notifications off on your phone. By your afternoon history class, @GuyInYourMFA has more followers than your primary account. By the end of the week, it has 3,000. Two weeks and 10,000 followers later, you'll see an angry tweet from someone who looks vaguely familiar. "Hey! You're using my picture for this account, WTF!"

You are definitely, and almost assuredly illegally, using his picture (you had done a Google image search for "guy in hat" and gone with the best candidate). You apologize, profusely, and that afternoon you bring a slouchy hat you own to meet your friend Simon in the library, the same library where you took your Introduction to Fiction class, and you ask him to stand there, against the shelves, and you take a hundred pictures of him with your cell phone and replace the picture of the stranger by that afternoon.

You tweet as many times a day as your brain allows. You gorge yourself on praise and the constant, steady companion of the "new notification" marker. You become the pop phenomenon of the week, a digestible trendy token of Internet culture for the in-the-know to consume and share.

"Maybe this girl with the tattoos can save me," reads one tweet.

"Every Friday is Black Friday when you're a nihilist like me." (Of course he would be a nihilist—of course he would love calling himself a nihilist, using the word as often as possible.)

"I wrote this poem for you on a cocktail napkin. Did you read it already? So fast? No no, really READ it."

You type the tweets as fast as you can think of them. Like an actor using a certain anchor phrase to practice a foreign accent, once you had certain anchor concepts about this character—a love of black coffee and cigarettes, an obsession with David Foster Wallace, general misogyny—you can find a way to riff on any topic. It is effortless. And if the attention you had been getting from your normal Twitter account is akin to a buzz like caffeine, this account is heroin. You can't look away from the way the notifications endlessly compile at the top of your screen.

But the best day comes two months later, before your acting class (you're a senior; seniors get to take acting classes), while you're sitting in the hallway balancing your laptop on your knees, staring at your account and rereading the tweets you've already done, trying to mine them for new inspiration. "Oh shit," comes a voice above your shoulder. "Are you reading Guy In Your MFA?"

"Hah," you say, "yeah." Technically, the account is anonymous, but your identity is an open secret. All of your friends, anyone you've talked to at a party, and anyone who read your profile in the *Brown Daily Herald* knows it's you. And now this boy, with shaggy hair that comes down to the top of his ears and a knit cardigan, knows you too. You know him—you've seen him at parties and in plays. You know him and now he knows you.

"I love that account. It's so dead on." He lets his backpack droop onto one shoulder and you smile. He doesn't know. He doesn't know it's you. This must be why celebrities wear baseball caps and sunglasses in public—not to avoid paparazzi or attention, but to *control* attention. For this feeling, the power to reveal.

"Hah, yeah," you say.

"But I feel like you kind of have to be a guy to understand all of the humor," the acquaintance continues. "Like, it's mocking this super-masculine experience, this thing that we're supposed to embody."

Whatever words you'd planned on saying, the metaphorical cape you had been about to sweep back, revealing your genius self, all disappear in a poof. Your eyes widen and you grin. "Yeah," you say. "Guess I will never get it."

And you close your laptop and walk as quick as you can down the hallway and into your classroom even though you're fifteen minutes early, because if you'd stayed there even a second longer you would have succumbed to temptation and ruined the whole, perfect, delicious thing.

YOU LOOK AT THE FLOOR WHEN YOU ENTER THE MINI-MART AND FOCUS ONLY ON THE SHELVES, loading your arms as heavily as you can without embarrassing yourself by scattering everything on the floor—no one wants to be the fat girl in stained sweatpants who sent peanut M&M's scuttling across the linoleum.

Your eyes jump rapidly between labels the way a close-up of a drug addict's eyes would in a movie. Prepacked peanut butter cookies, Cheez-Its, peach-flavored gummy rings, Ho Hos, family-sized bags of Doritos, pistachio nuts, a pint of ice cream, a Kit Kat bar—foods you forgot were edible when you were fastidiously logging your calories. You try to purchase enough variations so that you can order your consumption sweet-savory-sweet-savory. In addition to this rule, a "sweet" peanut-based product—say, a Reese's Peanut Butter Cup—shouldn't be neighbors with a savory nut product, like the bags of unshelled pistachios you would pour into a mug and then unhinge, one by one, with fingernails made so thin and brittle that they sometimes cracked and peeled from the exercise. The idea is to introduce as much variety into your binge as possible so that you won't be fatigued twenty minutes in.

Avoid eye contact with the checkout girl—it's always the same one, with her thick, cheap blond streaks and the piercing through her eyebrow and the hint of mockery (isn't that a hint of mockery?) in her voice when she asks, "Will there be anything else?" Maybe she thinks you're buying all of this for a party, you think limply. The family-size bag of chips, the sleeves of Milanos, those could be for a party. The same one you've been throwing every night this week.

"Uh, yeah," you say, and reach down below the counter to supplement your bounty with whatever candy bar is most appealing for you to unwrap on your way back to your dorm room, something to chew on for three blocks.

You hand over your debit card, still avoiding eye contact, and, yes, you'll need a bag, thank you, sign the receipt still looking down, and then you're gone, your shameful goods safely hidden behind opaque black plastic. Those are the worst moments, while you're in the store, when the binge is on the counter, when anybody could walk in and see you and you try your hardest to be invisible.

The concept of being addicted to something has always been elusive to you. Why couldn't they just, you know, stop? Sure it's hard, but just...do it. Don't do the thing that you know is bad for you. And then you let yourself eat after slowly starving for eighteen months, and you understand.

It's a chemical calling, a wiring in your brain that nags and tingles until you can only think about how good it would be, at that moment, if you could have a pint of ice cream in your lap, an entire pint, and an endless amount of food, never running out, for you to put in your face while you watch videos on the Internet. The world is so boring, and it's better if tonight you can eat whatever you want in an endless amount, isn't it? Everything you want. As much as you want. Just this once. It's a desperate, skin-tingling itch. A melody one note short of completion. Your mind keeps going back to wanting it so bad like water swirling a drain.

Because, of course, this is going to be the last time. You are going to get it all out of your system, eat *everything* you've ever wanted, because if this is the last time, you're going to need to try one of everything so you don't want it later. Just go. Just go to the minimart. You don't even have to put on a bra or makeup, just a big coat and a small, hidden, blank face. It doesn't matter if it's raining or if it's snowing or if it's the blizzard that they canceled school for and your mother is calling you to make sure you're okay—you just need to get the black bag full of the things that will dull the ache in your stomach.

You keep it a secret as best you can, but it comes out sometimes in ragged edges: parties where you can't stop eating the chips and salsa in the center of the table, evenings with friends where you're so focused on the pizza, first its presence—Are we ordering pizza? When will it get here? Has someone ordered the pizza?—and then eating as much of it as possible while still maintaining what you hope is an air of casual, normal twentysomething indulgence, that you can't think of anything else. You leave early, always, to go home to your bed and your laptop and your filling yourself up until you don't have to think about anything else.

You are a junior in college and you go home to the Chicago suburbs for winter break. It's a respite of clean sheets and fresh coffee in the morning. You get kisses on the head from people who pretend not to notice how much weight you've gained. But more importantly, it's the latest artificial deadline you've created for yourself, because "I'll stop doing this when I go back to school" became "I'll stop doing this as soon as classes officially start" became "I'll stop doing this as soon as finals are over," but you never stopped. Going home will be the habit breaker. You remember reading somewhere that you need a change of scenery sometimes to break habits because it disrupts your routine. You won't be two blocks away from a minimart that offers infinite permutations of sugar and trans fats, and your childhood bed is not one in which you would ever fall asleep watching YouTube videos with a half box of cereal spilling across the sheets. It would be different, and you would be safe, and go back to school twenty pounds lighter with clear skin and the discipline to work out every morning.

Your doe-eyed optimism lasts one night. Your second night home, you make yourself a bag of popcorn while your family watches *Dateline*. Air-popped, kernels measured out by the teaspoon, completely acceptable under your mother's watchful eye. But then the chewing reignites the stirring of a familiar animal.

"Mom, do we have any desserts in the freezer?" you ask. It's totally normal for a college kid to want to snack on desserts. It's practically cliché: college kid looking for junk food in a house that her mother keeps infuriatingly carb-free.

"I think we might have some brownies in the drawer," your mom says.

There are brownies, and you microwave one on a paper towel and while you eat, you perform a one-woman show about how delicious it is, and how good it is to treat yourself every once in a while, and dessert is okay in moderation.

The rest of the family goes upstairs, turning off half the lights along the way and leaving long shadows on the tastefully decorated French-farm aesthetic kitchen. And it begins without you even needing to make the conscious decision, a perverse opera, a scene from *The Nutcracker* in semidarkness but instead of flitting about presents on pointed toes you rummage through the cabinets for anything you can consume quickly, anything that will satisfy whatever terrible habit you've created for yourself. Endless bowls of cereal (never finishing a box, distributing your scavenging among the variety, always leaving enough so no one can tell you took it); pseudo-healthy nut bars, their sticky wrappers buried so far in the kitchen trash no one will find them; half a dozen English muffins microwaved and smeared with butter and raspberry jelly; leftover pasta eaten cold from the fridge by the handful. When you are satisfied, or in pain, or left with nothing that appeals to you, you crawl upstairs.

Sometimes you try to throw it up: curled over the toilet like Gollum from *The Lord of the Rings*. Bulimia turned you into Gollum in a lot of ways—the conversations you have with yourself ("Maybe you could just take a walk, or a shower instead of doing this whole binge-purge thing again?" *"Filthy habitses!"*), the hoarding of your food like it is your Precious, and the way you look when you come up from vomiting—face ruddy, eyes bloodshot, hair hanging in stringy clumps. Andy Serkis would nail you in a motion capture role.

Maybe all eating disorders are secretly characters from *The Lord of the Rings*. Bingeing turns you into a hobbit, thrilled by comfort and staying at home and coming up with as many excuses for meals as you can. A Bilbo Baggins: stout and antisocial and eating breakfast, second breakfast, and elevensies. And back when you were eating 400 calories a day, seventy pounds lighter and dreaming in calories, you definitely thought of yourself as an elf: thin, spry, delicate, and beautiful, but really, such an asshole when you think about it. I mean it was such a jerk move for the elves to leave Middle Earth on a giant ship when Frodo just worked *so hard* for three goddamn movies to save it. They're just like, "Thank you for your hard work, I guess, but we were already planning on peacing out, so..." Beautiful, pointy-eared jerks.

But, alas, now you have become Bulimia Gollum, and you deserve to live in a cave where no one will have to see you.

It lasts like this at home for a week, a nightly ritual of a silent gluttony, witnessed only by the dog, scratching and whining in her crate, woken by the beeping of the microwave. Your hidden, terrible secret. The secret that you are transformed in the night like Dr. Jekyll into everything you wish you weren't: out of control, unhealthy, indulgent, fat.

And then, one morning, things are different.

You come downstairs and your mom and dad are dead eyed and silent, standing together on the other side of the counter. And on the counter are the near-empty bags you've left hidden in the back of cabinets: the cereal boxes with only crumbs left, family-sized bags of chips that have gone from full to empty in the time you've been home, dozens of wrappers pulled out of the trash, hidden Ziploc baggies that once held a dozen brownies you thought everyone but you had forgotten.

They didn't say anything because they didn't need to. You, for your part, went through all the stages of a washed-up celebrity on an intervention show. You deny, you pretend, you accuse, and then, when there is nothing left to deny or pretend or accuse, you cry and you concede. Maybe you don't need to bear the secret burden. Maybe this bingeing is like a tumor that fixed itself to your brain, a medical malady that needs outside attention. Maybe it isn't entirely your fault. Within minutes, you go from the character of steely

Ivy League go-getter to sobbing inpatient who just gave up. Okay, okay, please help me.

There is no magic solution. There's no answer. You discover with tremendous guilt the next day that your mom cleared most of the food out of the cabinets, your regular binge food. Your parents watch you carefully. You oscillate between optimism and thrashing, guilty depression. Mostly, you just want another fix.

It never goes away, not really. You get better, you eat less when you feel the urge, and the urge comes less often. You lose twenty pounds slowly and feel a bit better about photographs of yourself. But even now, writing this, your head hurts from the salt of the Chinese food you ordered with the small thrill of a misbehaving child, choosing fried dishes and pork dishes because they somehow still seem forbidden. Your brain still isn't always on your side. All you can do is learn to live with the enemy, the begrudging respect of the police chief and criminal in a murder mystery, when they make long-awaited eye contact and nod at each other. *We might not always see eye-to-eye*, that nod says, *but goddamn it, I can at least acknowledge you.*

You're entering the living room of a friend's house on campus when you see a stranger there, already laughing, surrounded by people. That's not unusual: Alumni frequently come back to visit, sending an email out to friends and letting them know that they'll be in the neighborhood. Usually they're not more than a few years out, so the older students still remember them, but once or twice potbellied men with shiny heads and pleated khakis ring the doorbell and look around, seeming a little bit dismayed that we didn't all somehow remember them.

This stranger looks young, maybe two or three years out of school, but you don't recognize him. High cheekbones, clear light skin, and very blue eyes. He looks a little bit like an Adonis, a marble statue of a sinewy athlete with long limbs and a pretty face, but leaning more, you think, toward Benedict Cumberbatch.

"You," you say by means of introduction, "look so much like Benedict Cumberbatch." This being 2012, neither he nor anybody else really knows who Benedict Cumberbatch is. "You know, the guy from *Sherlock*."

There are a few murmurs of half-recognition but no one really gets it.

"Come on. You know!" you try again, and then noting the blank faces, you pull up Google images on your phone, scrolling mostly until you find a good picture of the Cumberbatch with similar light brown curls. "See?"

"Yeah, I see it," someone says, but you're waiting for the stranger's verdict.

He looks at you, a half-smile across his lips (he's the only man outside a clichéd screenplay who can actually pull off a half-smile) and he says, "Definitely."

He's looking at you and smiling and now you want to know everything about this stranger. This handsome, older stranger with the perfect face who appeared with his hands in his pockets in the foyer of a home like a suitor in a Jane Austen novel. You study him, and you see the thick silver band around his ring finger, but it maybe has a Celtic pattern on it, and then you see him smiling at you again and you know he almost definitely, probably, isn't married.

You pull up his Facebook profile discreetly on your phone just to see if you can discover, if not a wife, then maybe a girlfriend. There's no relationship status, although there are a few photos of him in a suit, dancing with a woman who might be in a wedding dress but also might just be in a dress. "Hey, Grace," you say, pulling one of the older students toward you. "Is that alum guy married?"

"Yeah, I think so, actually," she says. "Why?"

"Oh, he just seems so young," you say, hoping the disappointment in your face doesn't come through.

"I mean, he's in his thirties," she replies, and rejoins people talking in gossipy clusters.

So, probably married. You take a deep breath. That doesn't mean you can't spend time with him, talk with him, do some harmless flirting. And so you join the conversation. You listen to him talk about books you've never read and try to interject with remarks that you hope are winning and witty. Your favorite thing about him is his voice. It's soft and lilting but very deep, with vowels that curve around with patrician, almost British-sounding Received Pronunciation. Even surrounded by people, Married Guy keeps making eye contact with you and smiling. The two of you keep finding excuses to pull each other aside. It's almost like he thinks you're special.

"Have you heard the podcast *Welcome to Night Vale*?" you say to him finally. He's talking about H. P. Lovecraft and how Providence's prince of horror was buried in a cemetery not too far from campus. "You'd love it," you say. You already know what he'd love. "It's like H. P. Lovecraft meets slightly steampunk conspiracy theories meets...Jack Handey."

He hasn't heard any of it, and you have it on your phone, and the two of you pull away, down the stairs until you're sitting side by side in the basement. You retreat into darker and darker corners as people keep walking through and interrupting, until the two of you are in a back room—a library-cum-storage-closet—on a sunken half-broken couch, almost touching in near darkness. The two of you share a pair of headphones and listen to one full episode of the podcast, both with a performative look of concentration. So he's married, but that doesn't mean you can't flirt. In fact, it probably means you should be flirting, because it just sets the game's parameters. He can't do anything; you make him want it. Older men are supposed to fall in love with lively college co-eds who make them realize that they need to be living life to the fullest or something. You've read *The Western Canon*. There was a Josh Radnor movie about that, wasn't there? If you can't make him want you, then it's a massive failure on your part.

When the podcast is done, he removes his bud from his ear but he doesn't stand up.

"Have you read Lovecraft?" he asks. You haven't. Usually you lie about this sort of thing when a cute boy asks, especially at Brown. Never show your weakness, that you don't belong. But with Married Guy, you want him to know everything. You can't lie to him. You just shake your head and he smiles.

He stands and paces the room's bookshelf walls until he finds what he's looking for, seizing it with a triumphant, "Aha!" It's a book of Lovecraft, of course. "You showed me something, and now I get to show you something."

And so the two of you sit, now alone in a room surrounded by hundreds of books and mismatched furniture,

a collection accumulated by decades of students contributing what they no longer wanted or couldn't pack at
the end of the school year, and Married Guy opens up a
book of H. P. Lovecraft and begins to read aloud to you a
story called "Nyarlathotep."

It's all purple prose, horror movie nonsense really, but you
don't care. You can barely concentrate on the story so distracted are you by his voice, that voice you loved from the
start, and wondering whether you could rest your head on his
shoulder or whether that would be crossing some invisible
line. You lean your head in anyway, so you can read over his
shoulder.

"'And I saw the world battling against blackness; against
the waves of destruction from ultimate space,'" Married Guy
purrs, and you let your pinkie graze his.

He's one of the most handsome men you've ever seen in
person, maybe the most handsome. In profile, you can make
out the perfect lines of his profile and Lord Byron curl. His
skin is so pale he practically glows, inhumanely devoid of
any blemishes or imperfections. Just being this close to him
makes you feel electric, a pulsing slug of adrenaline with its
origin source your hand, just barely touching his skin. And
he's choosing to spend time with you.

"'Trackless, inexplicable snows, swept asunder in one direction only, where lay a gulf all the blacker for its glittering
walls,'" he growls, and you put your whole hand on top of
his, scratching softly with your fingers.

Married Guy hesitates, closing the book but keeping his
place. "Dana," he says. "You are so sexy. Really. And honestly, if I weren't married I would be flirting back with you
so hard right now you have no idea."

You pretend to be insulted. "Flirting?" you say. "This is just how I normally act. I wouldn't be flirting with you."

And maybe he believes it, because he keeps reading.

"'Screamingly sentient, dumbly delirious, only the gods that were can tell,'" he murmurs, and now you are all but nuzzling him, your head resting in the crook of his neck, your hand almost fully in his. He doesn't move to welcome you, but he doesn't stop you either.

Finally, he finishes. And the book is closed, and the two of you have no more excuses to be alone in a darkened basement room. You can't let this moment end. Everything else in your life is out of your control—you live at the whim of your cravings and your impatience, but if you say the right things tonight, you'll get to spend more time with this stranger who makes you feel wanted and seductive in a way you always dreamed you could be.

"Let's go to the cemetery," you say. "Let's spend the night. Come on; I've never been there." Your blazingly bright phone screen says it's almost midnight. It seems incredibly romantic to sneak into a cemetery at midnight.

"I cannot," he says, sounding like a Shakespearean protagonist. "I am exhausted."

"That's no fun," you say. "Come on, you only live once, and all that. How much longer are you in town?"

"Not long actually," he says, looking directly into your eyes. You feel the creeping heat between the two of you and you drum your fingers on your thigh to keep from wrapping your arms around him. "Leaving tomorrow."

He must read the disappointment in your face because then he says, "But I'll be back. You'll see me again."

"Promise?"

"I promise," he says. And the two of you stay in that room, broken off like an escape pod hurtling through space away from the rest of the house, from the rest of the school, from the rest of your lives. And then one of you opens the door and it all comes rushing, screaming back.

Turn to page 74.

YOU DON'T THINK YOU'RE DEPRESSED, but then again you also didn't think that you had an eating disorder even though you spent 85 percent of your brain power calculating and recalculating how many calories you consumed or planned to consume on any given day.

If you were depressed, would you be able to rationally question whether you were depressed? It's the catch-22 of mental illness: How can your brain not be working right if you're as goddamn self-aware as you are?

But then again, there were the nights in high school you spent sobbing so hard you were gasping for air on your bathroom floor, your face pressed onto the cold tile. You like the idea of killing yourself but hate the idea of being dead. You just want to not exist. Would that be possible? Who could you see about arranging that? The groove between the tiles leaves a ridge in your cheek. If you could just stay there forever, that would basically be like disappearing. You could just never move and starve to death unless they force-fed you, in which case you would stay alive as long as they thought it was worth it. You could literally just stay on the floor forever and never move no matter what anyone tells you to do.

The truth is you don't really know why you're crying. You just cry now, almost all the time, and for no reason. It's as though a reservoir of tears had been accumulating for a drought throughout your entire body and now some lazy intern at the water reservoir has accidentally leaned on the OPEN DAM lever.

That had happened once your senior year of high school. You had locked the bathroom door mostly to be dramatic, but when you heard your parents murmuring on the other side about breaking it down, you forced yourself up from the floor, clicked the lock open, and returned again to the tile before they could get in, as if the door had been unlocked the entire time. You're still sobbing.

"Do we take her to the hospital?" your mom asked.

You sobbed louder. You didn't want to go to the hospital. If you didn't do anything, if you just stayed there sobbing on the floor, then they couldn't take you to the hospital.

Your dad tried to help you up and you liquidated your muscles like a rag doll.

"Noooooooooooooo," you managed to get out between gasps.

"What do we do?" your parents asked each other.

"Noooooooooooooo," you moaned, and your sobs became even louder. You were making a spectacle of yourself and you didn't know why. It was as if the black pit of teenage angst in your soul could be excised like a demon if you cried loud enough and long enough and acted like enough of a hassle to everyone in your life so that they would eventually have to leave you alone. It was only when your dad managed to pick you up and began to pull you down the stairs ("Don't hurt your back, Michael!") that you realized they did intend to put you in the car and bring you to the hospital and that that was something you wanted to avoid at all costs.

You were still sobbing but the words you were able to garble out through the snot changed: "Please, no, no, no. I'm better now. I'll do whatever you want." Over and over again. "Please, no, no, no. I'm better now. I'll do whatever you want." You will see as many doctors as it takes. You will eat the Mallomar cookies and glasses of whole milk your parents carefully set in front of you. You will get fat; you don't care: You hereby renounce ownership of your body. You were contemplating killing yourself. Becoming pliable to whatever recovery efforts your parents hoist onto your person can't be worse. In that moment, when you were eighteen, you felt so certain that you would recover. But an hour later, when the crying dried up and you got the oxygen back to your brain, that certainty had evaporated. Recovery felt a thousand miles away, uphill across a gravelly desert with no rest stops along the way and no cell signal. Your parents let you go to college because by then you seemed fine. Sometimes you were fine, but fine is not the same as better.

You know the animated *Beauty and the Beast* movie you watched over and over as a kid? Remember how even though it was the Beast who turned away the enchantress-beggar woman back when he was a prince, she punished everyone who worked for him too? The Beast got turned into a Beast, which was bad, yeah, but at least his general shape was humanoid. His servants became clocks and chairs and flatware, which never seemed fair; they didn't do anything wrong and now the Beast (did he ever get a name?), whose fault all of this was to begin with, gets to wear clothes and eat at the table and in general enjoy a basically human existence just with a little more fur and much bigger muscles while they're trying to figure out how a candlestick is supposed to go upstairs. But they don't leave the house. They don't revolt or band together or form a new furniture-only government. They just keep on being servants, doing the best they can as goddamn furniture, serving the guy who got them turned into furniture and who has been making no effort to unturn them into furniture. *Just leave!* you wanted to shout through the screen. *Why are you serving him food??* They're just going about their normal routines as if they don't realize they're now goddamn pieces of wood and metal. It makes no sense. Anyway. That's what being depressed is like. For some reason, you've transformed into this inanimate object version of yourself and everyone else seems to be functioning perfectly normally, keeping jobs and falling in love and passing tests and they expect you to do the same. "But I'm a coffee table now!" you want to shout. "There's no way that I, a coffee table, can get out of bed to study for a bio exam. That's not a thing coffee tables are capable of doing!"

And then someone who is not a coffee table will say something like, "My cousin started running marathons, and it made her mornings *so* much more productive. Honestly, I feel like if you could just start training, even twenty minutes a day, your sleep would improve; your mood would be better—it's like magic."

"But I am a coffee table!" you want to shout back into that person's smug, stupid face. "I cannot do the thing you are telling me to do!"

But instead you nod seriously and say, "Oh, totally," and then go about your life trying as best you can to do the things a human is supposed to do even though you aren't a human anymore.

When you are forced again from the safety of the bathroom floor, they take you to see a psychiatrist who has pharmaceutical brand names on his pens and on his prescription pad. He meets with you for fifteen minutes, you and your mom in chairs opposite him at his desk, and then he hands you a fistful of Lexapro samples and an order for you to pick up more when you need them.

The next psychiatrist will look at you aghast when you tell her what you've been taking. This one meets you at an office across the highway from an outdoor shopping mall. She shares this office with a marriage counselor and a child psychiatrist. There are always crying people in the waiting room flipping through weeks' old issues of *People* magazine.

The third one meets you in her living room. The fourth meets you in his basement. You try to remember why you're going through this in the first place (it's because you were having "suicidal ideations" on your bathroom floor). It all seems like such a hassle for things to feel like they're barely getting better.

The pills don't affect you, not at first. You're hypervigilant, waiting for the effects to kick in like the soundtrack of a movie—suddenly a rush of chemicals hits your brain and you'll be happy. "It's like the sun is always shining brighter," your brother tells you when you come home bearing the crinkly pharmacy bag. He was on this brand of antidepressants, too, until he took himself off them cold turkey one night and ended up at the hospital in a panic attack so bad your parents thought he was dying. "I just prefer to feel like myself."

You still feel like yourself, at least for now. Taking these pills reminds you of the time you ate half of the pot brownie that a friend of a friend had sold you from his mini-fridge for $20. You log your thoughts like you're a captain of a submarine marking the enemy position. Normal. Normal. Normal. Normal. Maybe waiting for something to change with a hypervigilance that negates any possible change. The pot brownie was a dull disappointment—not even dry mouth or a disorienting awareness of your thoughts being trapped in your head (you wonder now if they had been regular brownies all along).

But after one day of forgetting to take your pill, you become irritable and moody. You snap at the people you love and lose focus at work, checking your phone every fifteen seconds like an animatronic Disney character on a loop, clawing at the Internet for validation and distraction. After two days, the brain zaps begin.

You didn't come up with that phrase, *brain zaps*. You found it on a website after you Googled "cymbalta withdrawal symptoms electric shock no pain." It was right there, listed first among the grouping of likeliest side effects: *brain zaps, irritability, nightmares and sleep disturbance, diarrhea, aggression.* Seeing the seemingly inexplicable sensation explicated, neatly wrapped up into two words and offered emotionlessly on the Internet makes you less afraid. They say misery loves company—the same goes double for strange medical side effects.

Because you'd been afraid, when the zaps first started, when one morning of running out the door and forgetting to take your pill had become two mornings, and you are sitting at a desk in your Bio 0200 lecture and it suddenly feels as though your brain has dragged its feet along thick carpeting and then touched a doorknob. It's painless—perhaps that's the strangest part, that you get the *sensation* of an electric shock without any pain, leaving you unsure whether it actually happened, at least until the second and third zaps follow. When you try to describe it later to your mom (tentatively, casually, nonalarmist), it feels like trying to describe what "salty" tastes like. You're fumbling with a new sensation and without the proper vocabulary. You are describing color to a blind man.

Now that WebMD has given you the phrase *brain zaps*, you feel comfortably normal about it. It's just one of those things that goes along with being one of those people who take antidepressant and antianxiety medication.

And so you take the pills every day, right before you put on your deodorant (the irony there is if you forget one, it means you forget the other, and those days are both incredibly anxious *and* incredibly sweaty).

You don't cry anymore, but you don't feel like yourself anymore either. So start again. Start from infancy, get better, and rebuild an identity for yourself.

Who is your identity going to be?

A. The coquette. You're only young once, and you're presumably never going to be as attractive as you are now. Put all of those tips you learned poring over *Seventeen* magazine as a teen to good use and actually flirt.

Turn to page 81.

B. The adventurer. Who says you need to be divorced to pull an *Eat Pray Love*? You're an upper-middle-class white lady. You can *Eat Pray Love* if you want to.

Turn to page 90.

THE NEXT TIME MARRIED GUY COMES TO PROVIDENCE IS DURING YOUR SENIOR YEAR. The two of you take giant cups of tea to go from the coffee shop on the corner and walk the streets, talking mostly about how much you connected last time. *Had it only been that once that we met?* the two of you exclaimed. *I feel as though I've known you forever. What a spark we felt. What magic.*

The casting works perfectly. Benedict Cumberbatch and a young American newcomer playing intellectual soul mates bound together by sexual chemistry and a mutual love of macabre steampunk as a ten- (er, fifteen) year age difference and a pesky marriage threaten to tear them apart. Doomed lovers from the start. It's beautiful, in a certain way, if you can keep pretending that's how it is.

You talk about *Night Vale* again, and your crush on Neil Gaiman, and high-concept fantasy novels you've been meaning to read, but the conversation is so much more fun when it circles the drain, when you go back to your two-man *Romeo + Juliet*.

Married Guy comes back to the apartment you share with five other people, and he stands in the kitchen drinking a beer, pretending you and he are just friends. He comes back to your room and sits on the bed, and then lies on the bed until you're face-to-face and he leans in to kiss you. The temptation of him intoxicates you. You know how much he wants you, and this terrible game is more exciting than any you've ever played and now the two of you are kissing.

It's wet and amateurish. The explosion of fireworks, the

swelling of a John Williams score never occurs. It's just you and a thirtysomething man in your bed, awkwardly making out. *But this is Married Guy*, you think to yourself. Your doomed lover. There has to be something between you, or else what have you been talking about for the last two hours? When he pulls away, you surprise yourself with how much you want him to come back.

"I love you," he says.

"This is crazy," you say. "We've only met once before! We barely know each other."

"I feel like I know everything about you."

"Me too," you say, and you think you're telling the truth.

He stands up and pulls on his pants. Somehow his pants had come off.

"Stay," you say.

"I can't," he replies.

You flip your hair as sexily as you can and arch your back.

"I can't," he says again.

"I love you, Married Guy," you say, and with a pained, yearning glance, he leaves and says goodbye, that we're going to have to try and be good.

The next day, an email alerts you to the fact that he's gifted you a song on iTunes, and then another. They're mournful songs over techno beats, sung by warbling altos. One was called "Women Scorned." Another had the lyrics "You're no good for me, but baby I want you." He sends you a song about a passenger making his last phone call aboard a crashing plane. You make a playlist and listen to them over and over again, persuading yourself to cry into your pillow for your love story cut short.

He emails you two months later.

I can't stop thinking about you. I'm more than a little jealous keeping up with all of the exciting things you're doing on Twitter (or seem to be doing? It's hard to tell where online personas stop and real life begins). Last time I was in London, there was this graffiti I remember seeing scrawled in the men's room of some pub:

The legions of Lilith, thrown out of Eden to meet the Morning Star, for that is the land we inhabit.

I don't know why, but for some reason it makes me think of you. Anyway, this is a roundabout way of me saying I'm coming into town soon—beginning of October soon, and I was wondering if you might want to meet me for dinner.

He signs the letter with love, and his first initial.

What do you do?

A. You don't go. Of course you don't. Your little fantasy has run its course, and it's time for him to get back to his life of being the type of married thirtysomething who tells college kids he loves them. Say a silent prayer for his wife, and focus on healthy, tangible steps to make yourself happy instead of the brief, destructive ego boost that comes from his attention.

Turn back to page 32.

B. You go. You wear a fitted, long-sleeve top and a miniskirt with tights and boots with a stiletto heel even though it's icy outside and you're more likely to stumble to his car than gracefully enter with the Brigitte Bardot vibe you were going for. You'd pressed a credit card against the corner of your eye to make your plum purple eye shadow into as neat of a wing as you could. You put on lipstick.

You worry, when you do eventually manage to (gingerly) get into his car, whether your effort made you feel more "prostitute" than you intended. It probably has something to do with how awkward it is, the two of you, actually face-to-face, when you'd spent the last two months playacting as desperate paramours.

"How are you?" he says after kissing you on the cheek. Neither of you sure where the kiss was going to land.

"I'm good," you say. "You know, the usual."

Falling in love with a married man is not a complete disavowal of your character, you reason with yourself. Carrie Bradshaw was in love with Mr. Big when he was married. She even cheated on Aiden with him when Mr. Big was still married to his perfectly fine wife. Olivia Pope was the other woman. Rory Gilmore slept with Dean right after he tied the knot. You learn that Sally Jay Gorce has a married lover within the first ten pages of *The Dud Avocado* and it's supposed to make her endearing. Perhaps you're just the complicated anti-heroine of your own life.

You keep building this narrative for yourself for the entire car ride, of how you just got carried away, how of course, any college student would fall in love with a wealthy, cultured, older man who portends to be in love with her. *It's not your fault, no matter what you do tonight,* you say, absolving yourself of all guilt and the pesky burden of morality. *You're the innocent ingénue, a tiny, delicate flower,* you try to tell yourself. *Or a femme fatale. Seducing men is a fun and sexy thing to do to pass the time in between smoking a smoldering cigarette and uncrossing your legs.*

But, when you look over at his profile, his Adam's apple bobbing with the motion of the car, a patch of downy blond hair on his neck where he missed a spot shaving, you don't feel like the delicate flower or the femme fatale; you feel like Julia Roberts in *Pretty Woman,* except you have no idea how to drive a stick shift and there's no way you would look anywhere near as good as her in a blue minidress that connects to a crop top with just a little metal ring.

Your knee shakes up and down while the car snakes its way down icy hills, from College Hill down to Providence proper. Married Guy stills it with his hand and looks over at you, smiling.

"What?" you ask. He tells you that you're beautiful.

There is no parking when you make it down to the restaurant, but you, in full fly-by-night manic-pixie-college-girl mode, have a plan. "Just valet it at the restaurant next door," you say. "It's fine. It's not like they're going to notice, or care." He agrees, and gives his keys to the valet at the Italian restaurant a few storefronts from your actual destination. You, the adventurous lovers, pretend to enter the Italian place until the car is nearly out of sight before slipping into your actual destination: a tiny, gourmet spot with about a dozen seats total, all stools around a central bar.

You hang up your coats and settle into your seats, and the warmth. You have done it. You are lovers out to dinner together, where no one knows you and you can finally, if temporarily, be together. His hand is on your knee again as he looks down at the menu and orders you both a first glass of wine. There will be one glass of wine per course, you learn.

You lean into his warm shoulder and return the gesture of hand-on-leg.

Just then, the front door of the restaurant opens and the valet from the Italian restaurant appears, flustered and determined. You panic and contemplate hiding in the bathroom. Married Guy rises from his seat.

In front of a tiny restaurant filled with well-dressed Providence professionals, the valet tells you that you aren't allowed to leave your car with him if you aren't going to eat at the Italian restaurant. Married Guy apologizes and leaves—to move the car presumably. "Turns out, the wait was too long at the other restaurant," he says as means of excuse, a pretty good one on the fly, you think.

While he's out mollifying the valet with $5 bills and reparking the car, you check your phone, reread the one-page menu, and avoid eye contact with the man eating alone a few seats down. He must know that you two are having an illicit dinner. Everything about this screams midlife-crisis-with-precocious-college-kid. You're practically that Josh Radnor movie.

Married Guy returns, the magic of the evening shaken a bit, but nothing that can't be restored by a few glasses of wine and a parade of dishes with descriptive words like *compote* and *frisée* and *reduction*.

"See how the wine seems to stick to the glass?" Married Guy says, demonstrating by swirling his red wine for you. "Those are the legs of the wine, where it comes down. See?"

You do see.

"So before you sip, you're supposed to smell the wine, get a full appreciation for its body and its taste. The majority of taste is smell anyway," he informs you.

You smell, and you taste, swirling it on your tongue in the most sophisticated manner you can. Married Guy goes first.

"It's almost piney. Like a burnt fire. But I taste plum, and maybe even some anise."

You didn't taste any of that. "I feel like the strategy for wine tasting," you say, "is just naming three random things. First a fruit, then a type of wood, and then a random object. Okay, like, I taste...cherries...and... oak...and...clay."

"Hah," Married Guy says, but not actually laughing.

It's more fun to talk about yourselves anyway, to wonder in murmured whispers in ears whether the man sitting at the end of the bar knows you two are having an affair. You run your hand up his thigh so far you can feel his erection through his pants.

Dinner consists of dishes brought one after another, each announced by a waiter as he delivers it like he's presenting a member of the royal family.

You're asking questions, steering the conversation as far as you can go without driving off the cliff. Do you think you're going to have kids? Do you love your wife? When did you know you loved her? When did you know you wanted to get married? And then, when did you fall in love with me?

The answers are benign, only made exciting by his voice, by the fact you're talking about them, together, in public, at all.

The check paid (more than you spend on groceries in a month), you rise from the stool and brace yourself against Married Guy's arm. Does the man in the corner give you a look of disappointment or are you just imagining things?

Maybe he asks if you want to go back to his hotel, or maybe he just drives. Your hands are groping one another in the car like blind, desperate creatures.

You make your way through the lobby, telling yourself to feel like Julia Roberts alongside Richard Gere in *Runaway Bride* and not Julia Roberts alongside Richard Gere in *Pretty Woman* and you're in his room and you're in his bed and you're watching a movie because neither of you wanted to be the first one to lean in and kiss the other and you're just so, so sleepy from all the wine, wishing you could fall asleep but also wishing that you could be more awake for this, your last and only night with Married Guy, when he leans in and kisses you, a little sloppy and a little awkward and pulls himself on top and inside of you.

It's fine. He comes quicker than you expected. You get nowhere close. But still, in the morning when you're getting dressed, you think, *Fuck it,* and try to drive off the cliff.

"Come to Europe with me," you say. "I'm leaving for

three months after graduation. We'll spend every day in museums and restaurants and live there forever." As you form it, the plan becomes more and more desirable.

"If only I could," Married Guy says mournfully.

"But you can," you say. "Leave it all. Move to Europe with me." You scroll through the things that might be holding him back: his job? He can get a new one. His apartment? Sell it. His wife? He already slept with me. Get a divorce. "Let's do it. Run away with me."

"That sounds very, very nice," he says, pulling on a black dress sock (men getting dressed after illicit affairs are always pulling on black dress socks), "but alas."

His apathy infuriates you. You are willing to give him everything, your entire life, an adventure, and he's stuck in whatever lameness of the spirit has turned him into a thirtysomething sleeping with a college student. "Come on," you say again, already fully aware that you've crossed into desperate, that your efforts at persuasion are making you into a petulant child. "Hot chocolate in Paris, writing all afternoon on the Seine . . . " You aren't even planning on going to France, but the vision seems romantic.

Married Guy kisses you on the head. "You're going to have a really great time. I'm envious of you."

You don't have to be envious, you almost shout. *You could come!* But there's nothing left. No point. He drops you off at your apartment building, and you spend the day in bed, listening to the songs he sent you back when it seemed like he would've done anything to have you.

Turn back to page 32.

WHICH EUROPEAN CITY SHOULD YOU GO TO WHILE YOU'RE IN DEEP DENIAL ABOUT NEEDING TO ENTER THE REAL WORLD?

1. What's your favorite time of day?

A. Dawn, when the birds are chirping and the grass is laced with dew and woodland creatures are there to help you get dressed like you're a Disney princess. (Is this what dawn is like?)

B. Two in the afternoon. Prime napping hours.

2. What's the best way to experience another culture?

A. Making local friends who will show you where on the river all of the kids hang out because you're allowed to legally drink alcohol outside here.

B. Museums? Honestly, talking, let alone drinking in public, with random strangers is your personal nightmare. Are you supposed to just...go up to people? People who already have friends? It seems like planning to "meet new people" is a good strategy to end up "eating alone and looking like someone stood you up."

3. Which food is most appealing to eat for every meal?

A. Blood sausage, which sounds like the punchline of a terrible Popsicle stick joke about a vampire's favorite brunch food.

B. Chicken wings, because even in Europe you want everyone to know that you're not sophisticated enough to avoid getting barbecue sauce on your pants.

4. You're walking down the street and you see $100 just lying on the sidewalk with no one around who could have dropped it. What do you do?

A. Give it to a homeless person, or give it to the police.

B. Yeah, sure maybe you're *supposed* to bring it to the police or whatever, but you found $100 on the ground. Of course you just pocket it. Not to be selfish or greedy, but come on, you just found $100! You shouldn't have to feel *bad* about this, Quiz. Stop being a jerk, Quiz.

5. What gift would you want the most for your birthday?

A. A donation to your favorite charity.

B. What did we say before about making us feel bad about
    ourselves, Quiz? Stop being a holier-than-thou jerk. A
    leather jacket, okay? I want a really cool, nice leather
    jacket.

If you answered mostly As

You're going to **London**. Enjoy the land of Queen and Cumberbatch.

Turn to page 93.

If you answered mostly Bs

You're going to **Edinburgh**. All you really know about Scotland is that J. K. Rowling lives there and David Tennant is
from there, and honestly, that's more than enough.

Turn to page 106.

YOU'RE SHARING A HOSTEL ROOM WITH THREE DARK, VAGUELY MALE BLOB SHAPES OF INDETERMINATE EUROPEAN DESCENT. It's too dark to make out exactly who they are (the light in the hostel room is off because at least one of the dark, male blobs seems to be napping). You have already fucked up your European vacation by eating a bag of Jelly Babies from the vending machine in the hostel lobby too quickly, which you justified to yourself (poorly) by thinking, "I'm in the UK! Jelly Babies are not a thing in the United States! They eat them in *Doctor Who*. I'm *allowed* to binge based on this paper-thin excuse." And now you feel bloated and unattractive, shiny with sweat like a baby hippo, and your stomach oscillates between pain and nausea. You want to curl up into a ball and wait for your body to digest all the evidence of what you just did.

Your friend who you were traveling with has gone off to a club. Even under the best of circumstances, you hate clubs, and though maybe the aphrodisiac of "You're on a Eurotrip!" might have motivated you under different circumstances, nothing could compel you to put on something tight and spend the night standing around with too-loud music blaring when you're already one (or two) full bags of Jelly Babies in. Have a good time, you said. I'm not feeling well. See you in the morning.

And now you're alone, on your aching stomach, fat and self-loathing, in a city where you should be having fun and adventures when really you're just lying on a bottom bunk in a dark hostel room.

So you do what any girl does when she's desperate for attention and a connection to the outside world but unwilling to get out from under her covers: You log on to Tinder and update your profile with your most flattering pictures and an American flag emoji, and write as your description: "American girl, just passing through."

The magic of Tinder is, between uses, you always forget how god-awful it is. There's the inevitable parade of meatheads posing in front of dirty mirrors, the guys who think sunglasses are a replacement for a personality, the ones posing with a sedated tiger, the wannabe stockbroker types in shiny suits. And then on the off chance you find someone who looks halfway reasonable, you match with them, only for the first message to be something laden with the worst of all keyboard iconography: the smiley face with a tongue sticking out. Tinder is fun as a game, a please-please-choose-me, a chance to experience the brief thrill of talking faux-intimately to a stranger with whom you'll never interact again.

You want to go out, you do. You want to do *something*. Your stomach is feeling better. It's 7:30 at night and you're looking down the gun at an entire evening of being lonely.

You migrate to the hostel bar but it's more or less abandoned. You order a drink and stare at your phone. There's a notification from Tinder. From a cute boy you hadn't really spent much time on, with dark curly hair and kind eyes and a profile that reveals he likes literature. "This might not mean anything to you," he wrote, "and if it doesn't, just ignore it."

"Try me," you type back.

"I'm currently getting my MFA in creative writing," the text bubble replies.

You grin, alone, staring at your phone. He, this strange boy in a foreign country, knows you from Twitter, knows you started a joke Twitter account making fun of boys like him, boys who like David Foster Wallace and get their MFA in creative writing.

You want to type back a thousand exclamation marks, a heart, a kiss, an orgasm. You settle for a smiley face. "I won't hold it against you," you say. And you talk a little longer with this boy, whose name is Rory.

"What are you doing right now?" you write. "Want to get a drink?"

He does. And you do. You tell him where your hostel is, and he names a bar a block or two away. He'll meet you in an hour.

You try your best to get ready, you really do—brushing your travel-matted hair, smearing on whatever concealer hasn't yet melted in your purse to cover the pimples brought on by stress and sugar, pulling on the most slimming clothes you brought. Still, when you're waiting outside the bar, and he's one minute, then two minutes, and then five minutes late, you begin to wonder if he's even coming at all. Or, even worse, the nightmare scenario: whether he came, saw you standing outside, and left because you're so much more hideous in person.

Every boy that walks by *could* be him. You crane your neck and restrain yourself from shouting, "Rory?" at every brunette who passes. You check inside the bar, and then step outside again. One boy looks promising, but then he walks past. Oh God, he's going to just leave, isn't he? Are you that much worse than your profile pictures? The boy who looked promising is back in front of the bar, but he's not looking at you.

"Rory?" you try.

It's him. It's him, actually here. A little shorter than you imagined, but very cute in those thick-framed hipster glasses. Hellos are exchanged, and an awkward hug. You two enter the bar, side by side.

The bar is actually a neon-glowing pseudo-club, with pulsing music, ripped leather stools, and advertisements for evenings featuring names like "DJ Snakeyez" and "MC TITZ."

"Do you maybe want to go somewhere a bit more quiet?" you ask. He does, and the two of you walk, talking about books mostly, until you find a bar that looks like a teashop, all chintz and doilies.

Under his winter coat, he's wearing a knit sweater like he's goddamn Ron Weasley and carrying a canvas bag holding said books. He is better read than you, that much is immediately obvious, but he doesn't showboat about it. He seems very keen on impressing you, and you find that endearing. He is shy in a typical British way, looking down, apologizing, blushing, smiling. He answers the impertinent questions you ask from the side of his mouth. You like him immediately.

When he walks you back to your hostel, the two of you kiss before you enter, and you're surprised: You thought he didn't like you, or at least wasn't attracted to you. He must have just gone on this date with you because you were the girl he knew from the Internet. But the way he's kissing you now is so urgent and so innocent that it makes you really want him for the first time, not just in the abstract but in the *hold me, keep your hand on the back of my head, put as much surface area of your body as possible on mine and keep goddamn kissing me.*

"You know," he says to his shoes, "if you wanted, you could come back to my place."

"Oh, Rory," you say, and you know immediately, as if someone spoiled the ending of the night for you, that you don't end up going to his place.

He kisses you again. He does it well. He wants you to go back to his place. The tubes don't run this late. "We could just take the night bus," he says.

What do you do?

A. Go back to his place with him. Come on, you're only in Europe once.*

Turn to page 98.

B. Tell Rory good night and go back to your hostel.

Turn to page 100.

---

* (Okay, that's not actually true, but you're only in Europe once, now, at this moment.)

YOU REGRET YOUR DECISION THE MOMENT YOU AND RORY SIT DOWN ON THE NIGHT BUS. You're side by side, legs bobbing, staring out the darkened window, sharing the bus with only a few subdued drunks and a group of teenage girls hunched over their phones. The drive takes longer than you wish it would—every extra minute is another one you'll have to repay in the morning, to get back to your friend in the hostel at a reasonable hour, to let her know you're okay. You already told her that you were feeling better, that you met up with a friend and you're staying over at his place ("Rory, what's your address? Just in case") but she hasn't responded yet. What if she gets back to the hostel and assumes you're lost or kidnapped? What if you actually ARE lost or kidnapped? You glance at Rory but he only offers you a shy smile back and touches your leg. This is okay. You're being adventurous. No one gets hurt by being adventurous.

Except, it would seem, you.

Early this very afternoon, a piano delivery was scheduled to take place in North London for a television composer of mild renown who lived on a building's second floor. Upon realizing the stairwell was far too narrow to accommodate a grand piano, the movers engineered a rather ingenious hinge-and-pulley system to lift the piano up through the second-floor window. The piano was hoisted magnificently into the air only for the movers and the television composer of mild renown to realize with disappointment that the second-floor window was too small for the piano to fit through as well. Without additional instructions and with no other plan of action, the piano movers simply left, keeping the piano hoisted in the air so it would be, at least temporarily, safe from thieves and roving pianists until they could come back the next morning and figure out a way to actually get it inside.

While walking down the row of flats to reach where Rory is living, you are crushed by a falling piano that neither you nor Rory saw hovering above the walk like the sword of Damocles.

Your final thought is, *I hope someone goes through all of my old essays and fiction and publishes a book that rockets to bestseller status on the wings of my tragic backstory.* They don't, but Rory ends up writing a very moving short story about the experience.

THE END

Or go back to page 97.

IT'S JUST ALL TOO MUCH, thinking about going to a stranger's apartment by bus, having to come back in the morning—*torture*. Everything with Rory is almost exactly perfect, as if you'd conjured him—he's British, he's cute, he's literary, he's British—but you don't want to run away with him.

"I have my friend in the hostel, and I can't just leave her," you say.

"Yes, you can," Rory counters, and he's right, you know; you just could. You could say yes and go and work it all out in the morning but the stress and anxiety of the next day, at least in your imagination, is already pressing down on your body.

"I can't," you say. And you two kiss again, a little bit more, with a little less fire. "But," you say, "I'm not leaving London until Monday, if you wanted to hang out tomorrow or something."

"Yeah," Rory says. "Yeah, let's do that. I had plans to hang out with a friend—"

"Bring him," you offer. "I'm traveling with a friend from high school. We'll all hang out. It'll be fun." It might be completely awkward and terrible, but meeting locals is what the protagonists of Disney channel movies and YA novels are always doing. This will just be another fun adventure. You'll get some friends to show you the town on Vespas. "It'll be great," you say, with finality, and kiss Rory once again, almost on the lips but mostly on the cheek. You both give each other an awkward half-wave as you finally walk inside.

The next day, you and your friend Maddi meet Rory and his mate Cameron at Borough Market near the Tate Modern. Cameron is classically handsome, like that actor from *The O.C.*—Benjamin McKenzie. As he and Maddi shake hands, Rory makes eye contact with you and raises his eyebrows.

"I think we're meeting Jono and Claire in a bit," Rory says as the four of you weave between tables laden with home-made nougat and gourmet kimchi carts. "We can meet them up by the National Theatre." Rory and Cameron both consult a group text chain in their phones, labeled "The Gang." You just follow, dumbfounded, as, in less than an hour, Rory materializes a group of friends on the South Bank of London.

Claire is a graphic designer, with shiny hair and a round face that reminds you of a woodland fairy. "Oh, we've got to get Jono to come meet us," she says while the now five of you browse DVDs in the gift shop of a small film museum you've ducked into. Jono, you learn, is a bit like the gang's paternal figure, the benevolent force upon which friendships revolve. And so you're a little surprised when he arrives—grinning and bearded, with dark shaggy hair and an infinite supply of witty things to say, less of a mob boss and more of a very, very friendly dog in human form.

"You drink Pimm's?" Claire asks. You've never had it. "We have to get Pimm's. And then...hmm...what else is there for us to do?"

"South Bank book fair," Rory says.

"Ooh, and Borough Market," says Jono.

"We've already been there," says Cameron.

"All right, so we'll get some Pimm's outside the Tate—you two have been to the Tate Modern already, right? All right, good—and then the book tables," Claire says.

"Does that sound okay?" Rory asks you.

Yes, that all sounds really, really wonderful.

You spend the rest of the afternoon feeling as though you've dropped into a sitcom, a British sitcom in which four best friends who easily meet up anywhere in the city go on endless adventures together and build up an endless supply of infinite jokes. That was always the most unbelievable part of television shows to you—not the comically large apartments in New York City, or the designer wardrobes, or the perfect hair, or the revolving door of love interests: It's the friendships, that four or more adults can link their lives together so fully they become like family, never torn apart by moving away or someone getting a new significant other and spending the next six months in hibernation with them.

It's not as though you don't have friends, but spending too much time even with your closest friends from high school sometimes leaves you feeling desperate for a retreat back into solitude. Your friends in college were diverse and disparate. You always had someone to hang out with when you needed it, but there wasn't a group in which your inclusion was always a given. Rory and The Gang have been friends for years: Their anecdotes each have a different permutation of members involved but no one is the odd man out. They're all fully carded members of this circle they've created for themselves. They are all in the group chat.

At dinner that night, drunk on Pimm's and the subsequent bottle of wine, and on attention and the feeling of unqualified acceptance, you attempt a British accent. Terribly. "It's hard!" you say. "I feel like I can't do just the normal British accent that you all have. It's like in my head all Brits fall into one of two categories. There's the"—and here you lapse into

an almost offensive Dick Van Dyke cockney stereotype—
"'Oh, I'm a cockney chimney sweep! Tuppence, guv'na?'
and then there's the fancy people, like 'Oh, go sip your tea,
Madam Queen.'"

"SIP YOUR TEA, MADAM QUEEN!" the rest of the
table shouts, and erupts into laughter.

"Sip your tea, Madam Queen!" Claire roars.

"Or is it a command?" Cameron asks. "Like, you're
telling the queen to sip her tea: 'Sip your tea, Madam Queen,
if you wouldn't mind.'"

"I think the thing we're missing here," Rory says, "is that
no one actually calls the queen 'Madam Queen.'"

"I do," you say.

And you all start laughing again until your cheeks hurt
and you wish you could spend the rest of the summer pretending that you're one of them, that you share all of the
memories and were present for all of the stories.

You remind yourself that your admission into The Gang
is only a visitor's pass, as the girl that Rory went on a
Tinder date with and her friend. Even if you stayed in London, it would only be a matter of time before you faded
out and away. That's the terrible thing about friendship, real
camaraderie friendship that feels like family—it's not something that can be achieved like a level-up in a video game.
It's something you constantly earn, over and over again,
by virtue of just *being yourself* and somehow meeting the
ephemeral criteria.

But when you create your first inside joke with The Gang,
you feel good enough. Claire changes the name of the group
chat: SIP YOUR TEA MADAM QUEEN. All caps. It's what
she labels the album on Facebook where she'll post the

picture of you, caught mid-word but still smiling, because you had been smiling all day.

You and Rory will stay in touch, and you'll flirt and text and email your writing back and forth for months, a year, after you meet. Once, you will sing and play the guitar over Skype while he accompanies you on glockenspiel and secretly you'll imagine a version of your story in which you and Rory end up together. You'll imagine loving him, and you like how it fits. But you only talk in words on a screen anymore, and then, one day, both of you will meet someone else and fall in love for real and will have to tell the other person, a stranger across the ocean who you were never actually dating, that you're actually with someone else now. Whatever flame you two had, whatever nonrelationship, will be quietly folded and put away in the linen closet.

When you get back to the hostel that night, you have an email from someone at CBS. Remember that internship you applied for at *The Late Show with Stephen Colbert*? The one you wrote the gut-wrenchingly earnest cover letter for, practically prostrating yourself before the human resources intern assigned to sort through the messages from hundreds of similarly desperate college students?

Well, you got an interview. Can you be in New York in a week to come to the studio?

This internship, even the interview, is a once-in-a-lifetime opportunity. But then again, so is this trip to Europe. How long will it be before you get the chance to see Florence? Or Istanbul? Or Edinburgh? You were going to Edinburgh next. You need to decide your entire future now, at eleven o'clock at night, in the lobby of a London hostel where a group of strangers are laughing and smoking and drinking in a foreign language on the stairs a few steps away. You could call home, ask your mom or dad for their opinion, or ask Maddi, but what is anyone going to say that's going to be more important than the single most terrifying truth of all: *You should do what you want.*

So make up your mind, goddammit.

A. Book a flight back to the States for the interview. What's another European city of cheap hostels and cheaper beer? Just find a corner in the hostel kitchen where there's enough Wi-Fi to get you onto the Internet, and book a flight to New York City. You can stay on your friend Sarah's couch—she's still in New York for the summer. Your suitcase is already packed. What's the point of being spontaneous if you can't change your plans?

Turn to page 120.

B. Finish your trip. You're already here. When else in your life are you ever going to get the chance to tour through Europe with no commitments or responsibilities? If you go back and get a job now, that's it; this part of your life is over. It means you have a job now (even if it's a cool job) and you'll have a job until you retire. Hope you had fun being an unproductive member of society while it lasted.

Turn to page 106.

IT'S A FAIRY-TALE CITY, like there should be enchanted dwarves poking their heads out from beneath the sunny stones and iron banisters. Your taxi charges up steep inclines, weaving between ancient tilted buildings and sprawling parks and at every turn, at every new vista, you and Maddi look at each other with disbelief, delirious with the beauty of the city, with exhaustion from traveling.

The taxi sputters to a stop on a cobblestone street, just above the Royal Mile, where you can see the castle perched on a craggy hill in the distance. This is your hostel, with an iron entry sign hanging outside the door. Everything is already incredible.

The boy at the check-in desk doesn't look at you. He's on his phone, floppy hair over his eyes. "You guys checking in?" he says when he finally notices two exhausted girls in front of him, towing suitcases. His accent is Australian, and he has the whitest teeth you've ever seen.

"Uh, yeah," you say. "Should be three nights, under 'Schwartz.'"

When he hears your accent, the boy grins like a fox. "Americans, huh?"

"And you're ... Australian?" you ask. His looks and hostel job make it immediately obvious to you that this is a boy who frequently beds tourists. One of the perks, you imagine, of working in hospitality. Still, he's very cute.

"Right, so here's your room key, third floor. Bring your laundry to the front desk if you want it done. We have a sitting room around the corner and"—he gestures to a poster—

"there's a pub crawl tomorrow night." You and Maddi swipe your credit cards, take the keys, and head through the lobby, giving each other a look that says, *He seemed kind of sleazy, but definitely cute, right?*

You wonder if all Edinburgh hostels look like this. Are there wooden benches that resemble props from *Game of Thrones* and suits of armor in the hallway? Is there a kitchen, and movie theater, and a massive living area with couches and pool tables? This seems to be a place where people stay long-term. Someone explains you can book your room by the week and that if you take on cleaning shifts, they discount your rate. You offhandedly wonder how difficult it would be to uproot your life and stay here forever. Nagging words like *family* and *job* and *expensive flights* keep the thought from nestling permanently in your brain.

You and Maddi drag your luggage up two flights of stairs and enter your room. It contains about a dozen bunk beds, each in various states of use. A few people are napping; some are reading; some beds are still empty. The two of you find the beds you were assigned and wrestle your luggage into the corresponding locker. And then you look out the window and see the castle again, framed by the sunset, high on the hill that's half greenery and half stone. You've never slept in a room with a better view in your life.

The two of you head downstairs to the lounge area, where most people are engrossed in what appear to be personal and very important conversations.

You and Maddi look for an empty corner to sit in, maybe to begin researching what exactly you're supposed to do in Edinburgh, when you see one boy at an empty table, examining a bottle of whiskey.

You can tell he's American. You've picked up this skill after a few weeks of traveling, distinguishing between Australians, Canadians, Englishmen, Americans, Germans, based on the way someone stands or the way they're dressed. This boy exudes an almost pornographic familiarity.

"Where are you from?" you ask, already anticipating the answer: America.

"Chicago," he says, looking up from the bottle of whiskey at the two girls approaching him and smiling.

"Us too!" Maddi says. It's one thing to meet an American, with whom you immediately feel like teammates against the rest of the world, but someone from the same city, or even the same state, when you're thousands of miles away means automatic family.

"Where in Chicago?" you ask. You're from Chicago, too, as long as whoever you're talking to isn't *actually* from Chicago, in which case you're from Highland Park, a suburb some thirty miles north of the city proper.

"Buffalo Grove," he says. Another suburb.

"We're Highland Park."

"Oh, cool," he says. "Hey, you guys want to try some of this stuff?" He gestures to the stout amber bottle sitting across from him. "My friend and I bought it up in the Highlands when we were touring there yesterday." You can't help but size him up—he would've been cute by hostel traveling standards, but knowing he's American knocks that down a few points. He's tall but broad, with fluffy hair that makes him look taller, and brown eyes. A tattoo peeks out from beneath one of his shirtsleeves.

"My name's Bill, by the way," he offers.

Who would choose to go by Bill if they're not yet a thirty-nine-year-old divorcé? Bill is a name for car salesmen and stepfathers. If you have the choice to go by anything else, and you always do, you don't go by Bill. Even—yes—Billy is better if you're not a middle-aged man. But no. His name is Bill.

He pours three small glasses and gestures for the two of you to take them.

You take a polite sip. "I'm not sure I'm worth this expensive stuff because I almost definitely will not appreciate it."

If Bill was put off by your admission of ignorance, he doesn't show it. He continues to sip his glass of whiskey like he's taking Holy Communion, eyes closed, nose up, savoring every note.

The Australian who'd been working at the front desk enters the lounge area and scans over you and Maddi, settling his eyes on your friend. She meets his eye contact, and then gives you a look like, *What? He's cute; we're traveling.* You become aware of the bulge of flesh around your waistband and wonder if you could have done something about your appearance to make the Australian desk guy look at you.

You turn to Bill. "So what does your tattoo mean?" you say, invoking a *Cosmo* Sex Tip and gently touching the bird on his forearm to show him you're interested. His build—tall and wide but not overweight, as if his natural resting state is building a log cabin by hand—reminds you of a boy in your literary fraternity who you loved for one day in college, a boy who spent the night in your dorm room smiling into your ear and the next morning told you he was planning on asking out someone else.

Bill lets your fingers linger on his skin and smiles.

"It's a falcon. My dad has the same tattoo."

Maddi has already pulled out her phone, ignoring her glass of whiskey, foot tapping and ready to get out and explore the city, but you stay engaged for just a little bit longer. "That is really, really cool. Look, we're going to go out exploring and stuff, but maybe I'll catch you later?"

He bobs his head, almost agreeing but not quite. "Sure."

As you and Maddi fling yourselves out of the hostel and onto the cobblestones of the Royal Mile, she rolls her eyes. "Leave it to us to travel around the world and still meet a random weirdo from the Chicago suburbs."

You spend the morning huffing your way up one of the winding dirt paths to the top of Arthur's Seat, attempting to ignore the joggers high-kneeing their way ahead of you, swift and sweatless, while you drag your feet in what could only be described as a locomotive dirge while your lungs convulse for air.

But you make it to the top, and you see the city sprawl out under a churning, overcast sky, and you take a thousand pictures and then exhale and begin your uncoordinated descent.

The two of you dare each other to sip a single can of Irn-Bru a waiter laughingly brought to your table when he heard you were tourists who'd never tried it before. Through pursed lips, you identify the flavor: bubble gum. You leave the can, still full of bubbling orange liquid, on top of a trash can and follow a chalkboard sign to a restaurant serving a drink that appeals more to your American tastes: hot chocolate gelato floats.

By the time you return to the hostel, your hair is a halo of frizz and your sports bra is cutting into the flesh of your rib cage. "I desperately need a shower," you say.

"I desperately need a twelve-hour nap," Maddi replies.

"Pub crawl tonight!" the Australian guy pitches in from behind the front desk.

You and Maddi look at each other. You didn't come all the way to Scotland to turn down opportunities to drink.

Your memories of the rest of the night blink in and out of your mind like a strobe light. There the two of you are, following the group of tourists down a few streets to a bar that promises five-pound drinks to those of you with wristbands. There's Maddi flirting with the Australian. There's the Australian flirting with another tourist girl. There's you, shouting over the music that he's a piece of shit and that she can do so much better than him, and she's only attracted to him because he's there, not because he's actually all that cute. Then there's a second bar—one half empty, with a live band playing '80s rock covers, and then a third bar, this one outside and massive, with rows of long wooden tables like a biergarten. This one is crowded—you've lost Maddi but you've found a group of guys, all six foot or taller, all wearing kilts. And then you're holding a vodka soda and you find Maddi again and she's also found the group of guys who turn out to be a rowing team from Wales having a bachelor party of some sort, and then there's Maddi making out with the cutest one, the best man, and making me promise I'll be able to get back to the hostel safely alone because she wants to hang out with him a little longer, back at his place.

The strobe light effect ends there, and you're walking through the cobblestone streets, a map up on your phone but not really needing it—your hostel is at the top of the Royal Mile, just to the right of the castle. It's easy to find from almost anywhere in the city once you get your bearings, even when you're tipsy.

Bill is still in the lounge, as if he's never left. "Hey," you say, and he understands completely. You are immediately sitting on his lap, arms around his neck, making out.

"Let's go somewhere more private." His hand is around your waist and he leads you to the showers on the second floor—a white-tiled room that echoes only with the odd drip of water. He closes the stall door behind you and now, under the fluorescent lights, you're struck with the awareness that you're completely sober, and yet still here, with a stranger, in a hostel bathroom. "What's your last name?" you ask desperately.

He tells you while pushing you to your knees.

As he strips further, you become distracted by another tattoo, a familiar symbol on the left side of his stomach, slightly warped by a developing potbelly.

"What's that tattoo?"

"Oh," he says, looking down at it as if seeing it for the first time. It's a smiley face done in a faux-graffiti style, with Xs for eyes. "It's for Blink-182."

"Did you"—you pause and consider your words—"get it when you were a teenager?"

"No," he says. "Last December. Huge fan of theirs."

And so you finished a blow job in Edinburgh, eye-to-eye with the world's only unironic Blink-182 tattoo. You know unequivocally you will never be able to listen to "Adam's Song" again with a straight face.

"Let's go to your bed," he says, and begins leading the way, and even though you're almost positive bed-sharing isn't allowed in hostels, he's so sure of the idea that you follow along, sneaking through the darkened second-floor corridor. You creak into your room, shared by a dozen or so other travelers on half a dozen bunk beds. Maddi is sleeping, still in her clothes, on the bottom bunk—thank God. You and Bill yank yourselves up to the top bunk on the flimsy ladder, trying to be as quiet as possible, and you awkwardly maneuver until you fold yourself into a lowercase C in his arms.

You wake up to see him pulling on his jeans next to your bed. The sky is lit by the earliest morning outside your window. "You're leaving?" you whisper.

"Yeah, but let's get together before you leave town," he says. "I want to see you again."

"You never gave me your phone number," you say groggily.

"Don't worry about it," he replies, and he kisses you goodbye and slinks away before you have too long to think about what he just said, and you fall back asleep.

The next morning, the entire thing feels like a dream. You never see Bill again, never get his number, never find him on Facebook. In fact, like the end of a lazy ghost story, you never find any evidence of his existence at all. Once you tell Maddi about your evening, she joins you in the saga to find him somewhere online, first out of curiosity and then out of a stubborn fascination.

You know his first and last name. You know his father's name. You know where he went to college, and where he went to law school. You know what suburb he's from. And yet you've found nothing—not a Facebook profile, not a picture, no mention of him anywhere. You sail through dozens of pages of Google results. You try twenty spellings of his last name. Nothing. He was the ghost in your bunk bed, the haunting of the hostel, the manifestation of your lowest standards while traveling in human form. You imagine if you were to return to the hostel and ask the front desk if any guest had ever stayed there with that name, their face would go ashy and the reply would be, "That person hasn't stayed in this hostel for a hundred years!"

You could convince yourself the entire thing never happened, that it was a hallucination brought on by a mixture of Irn-Bru and cheap beer, if it wasn't for the memory of a Blink-182 tattoo, emblazoned in your brain like it had been emblazoned on his belly.

It's still a fairy-tale city, even Bill-less (perhaps especially Bill-less). "These are the streets that inspired J. K. Rowling to write *Harry Potter*," tour guides boast as you scan the cobblestone and crooked storefronts, eyes wide with wonder. Harry Potter lore is treated like a relic of Jesus himself. You make the pilgrimage to your holy sites. You force Maddi to set an alarm and make the trek with you to a small café on a Main Street outside Greyfriars Kirkyard. The Elephant House has a large red sign in its window with bright yellow writing: "BIRTHPLACE" OF HARRY POTTER. Inside, it's just a normal café, a good place for breakfast or a cup of coffee, but every chair and table hides a secret promise: Maybe *she* sat here while she was writing. The stalls of the bathrooms at the Elephant House are dense with writing, so much graffiti that you can barely make out the wall beneath. In less than a second, it becomes obvious what unites all of the scribbling: Some drew the deathly hallows triangle or sketched wands shooting off sparks. "I am writing this for Jeanine and Hannah Spencer who love Harry Potter," reads one note in pen, still visible under the red marker above it: "I solemnly swear I am up to no good." "Mischief managed," someone squeezed below it in different handwriting, but also in red.

You feel like an archaeologist, deciphering two decades of scrawlings for the series that pulled you into magic and that very restaurant. They're all notes of love and appreciation, and none have ever been painted over, just added to. You don't have a pen, but even if you did, you doubt you'd be able to find even a square inch of wall space to claim as yours. Even the wall behind the toilet back was dark with notes in every language. And so you just take a picture and head back to your breakfast. You're supposed to leave Edinburgh that afternoon—of course, the first day the temperature has crawled above seventy degrees. You still hadn't made it to the natural history museum or spent much time off the Royal Mile. The previous day you'd gone on a day trip up to the lochs, and, thanks to the 5:00 a.m. departure time, fell asleep almost instantly on the bus. But you had awakened to a world of green valleys and mist. Everything was wet and bright and mossy. Your bus wove across cursed bridges and around ink-black lakes lined with crumbling castle ruins. "I want to go on my honeymoon here," you announced to Maddi. "Just rent a cabin and live up here for a month." She didn't need to point out that you didn't have a boyfriend.

"How was the bathroom?" Maddi asks when you return to the table.

"Amazing," you reply. "You have to go see it. Covered with *Harry Potter* quotes. It's incredible."

"I love Edinburgh," she says, taking a sip of her latte.

"I could live here," you reply.

"Same."

"No," you say. "Really. I feel like I could live here."

"You should. I want to live abroad when I'm older."

"No," you say again. "Like, I feel like I could live here now. Maybe go to grad school."

Maddi raises her eyebrows. "I mean, University of Edinburgh is a good school," she suggests offhandedly. "And there's St. Andrews." Our friend Allison had shocked us all with her undergraduate decision to attend St. Andrews in Scotland, the mythical land where Will met Kate.

"I could get a job at the hostel and live there for free," you offer.

"You could," she says, half smiling, not quite realizing that she's due to call your bluff.

The rational part of your brain offers its polite rebuttal: You don't have a job here, and since you're not a citizen, you're not sure you'd be able to get a job. On the other hand, everyone working at the hostel was Australian or American. Your tour guide the other day was from Kansas, studying at the university. You could run tours and apply for graduate programs. You could ask your parents to ship some of your clothes, or better yet, you could start fresh, buying just what you need and living the minimalist, nomadic lifestyle you've secretly fantasized about while spending $60 at CVS buying makeup you already know you don't really like. You could start over again, in Scotland. No eating disorder, no depression. You'd run every morning and on the weekends take hikes on Arthur's Seat. You'd learn how to cook. You'd fall in love with a Scottish laird or a British academic. You would rebuild your life vertically from location up.

"What if I stayed?" you ask.

Maddi doesn't say anything.

What do you do?

A. Finish your trip and go back to the United States. You are not the "starting a new life" type of person. You would run out of money in Scotland. Why do people never think of things like that when they make the impulsive decision to live in foreign countries? Also, aren't visas a thing? Don't you need a visa? How do people get visas?

Turn to page 120.

B. You say goodbye to Maddi the next day when she takes a bus to London. You ask the front desk if you could apply for a job. They don't have a full-time job yet, but they let you work cleaning the kitchen and the living room once a day in exchange for half off your room. Turns out you do need a visa to get a job but not if you're just doing under-the-table work at a hostel and not, you learn, if you're a student. So you open a thousand tabs on your laptop for graduate school. You buy a six-pack of new underwear at the discount store on the corner. You do not have a European passport, or a closet, or a job, or a single friend, but you're staying in Edinburgh.

Turn to page 118.

THE SCOTTISH BOY YOU MEET TELLS YOU HIS NAME IS FERGUS. (You will find out later that it is actually Mike.) You met Fergus at a sticky-floored bar off the Royal Mile. He orders you a shot of whiskey without even asking and then gives you a crooked smile that you find irresistible. You ask him what he does. "Oh, this and that," he answers, which should have been your first red flag. But instead, you leave the bar and make out with him on the street while a tour group led by an American in a Mr. Hyde costume (eye patch, green face paint, top hat) passes by, gawking.

"Your place?" you ask.

"Nah, it's kind of far. Let's do yours."

"Ah," you say, between kisses on his neck. "So, unfortunately, I'm still in a hostel, and it's a shared room."

"That's kind of fun," he says, and winks. That should have been your second red flag. (The wink should have been your third.)

So you bring Fergus back to your shared room in the hostel.

The good news here is, even though Fergus is gone by the time you wake up in a newly destroyed hostel room, he didn't steal anything from you. With a raging hangover and a pit in your stomach, you pull the clothes that have been strewn across the floor back into your suitcase. He hasn't managed to find your money, or your passport, or your credit cards, which you kept zipped into a hidden compartment inside your purse.

The bad news is, your bunkmate—a girl named Emma from Texas—didn't keep her money, or passport, or credit cards zipped away anywhere.

You go with her to the American Embassy and pay her back $400. The hostel gives you an hour to pack your things before you have to check out for violating their no-visitor rules and Emma is told to buy a lock.

In the end, you return to Chicago mostly broke and very tired. Your hair is too long and stringy and before she even releases your hug at the airport your mom declares that you need to get it cut. It feels good to be taken care of again.

"I need to see the doctor this week, I think," you say.

You needed to get adventure out of your system—the fantasy that living in a different place will turn you into a different and better person. If Edinburgh couldn't do it, New York definitely won't. You start living at home, with your younger sister who's home from college for the summer, and the two of you fight and bicker like kids again until your mom insists you get a job and then you're working part-time at the local library and tutoring kids for the September ACT and you're saving up money but you don't know what for. (Emma emails and says the police were able to track down Mike, aka Fergus, and that she canceled her credit cards, and so you feel a little less guilty.)

Maybe you'll write a book, you think. But you can't even clean your room. Your mom has to remind you every morning to make your bed. How can you write a book if you can't clean your room? You are tired, and you are stuck, but you are safe. Maybe soon, once the last remains of your failed adventure are gone from your psyche, you'll be ready to try something new.

THE END

Or go back to page 117.

CONGRATS! YOU MADE IT TO NEW YORK CITY! ASIDE FROM LIVING IN AN APARTMENT WITH NO CENTRAL AIR BUT ENDLESS TAKEOUT CONTAINERS OF WHITE RICE IN YOUR FRIDGE, WHAT ARE YOU EXCITED FOR?

A. Having a kick-ass career. Since you are a lady, a successful career will always be "kick-ass," and the true measure of success will be how good you look in sleek black dresses and blazers and heels and how you can exit a car without ever flashing your underwear. Yours will be a world of glossy hair and expensive highlights and international flights and phone calls to people named "Mark" that you hang up on.

Turn to page 122.

B. Finding love. Isn't that what every New York City–based romantic comedy and television show promised? You are Carrie Bradshaw in *Sex and the City*, except you dress like less of a maniac and you don't wear heels to go to the bodega at two in the morning when you really, really need a pint of ice cream (you wear Birkenstocks).

Turn to page 132.

C. Meeting friends. A group of people that you can feel completely comfortable with, ideally a group with a standing weekly brunch date (see also: *Sex and the City*). The point of all friendships, you are mostly sure, is to see who can fit the most double entendres into the time between ordering omelets and brunch and the waiter delivering them.

Turn to page 152.

SEEING A CELEBRITY IN PERSON IS SOMEHOW ALWAYS BOTH MORE EXCITING AND LESS EXCITING THAN YOU IMAGINE IT'S GOING TO BE.
First, there's the first moment of recognition: "Is that them? No, it couldn't be. But it *looks* like them." That stage might only last a second before it's replaced by certainty. Yes, you got a good look at their face and there can be no doubt. This is the person you've seen on television screens and stared at on your laptop. And once you see their face— taller or shorter, fatter or thinner (usually thinner) than they appeared onscreen—the celebrity always looks shamefully like themselves, as if they just peeled themselves from a page of *US Weekly* declaring that they are "Just Like Us," because celebrities, too, sometimes shop for groceries using a grocery cart.

It is during this critical second stage that you must decide whether you're going to bother them. By the time your brain runs through all of the possible algorithms for interactions (ask for an autograph, ask for a selfie, tell them you loved their last movie even though you never saw it) but by the time you decide on a course of action, they're too far away, and the only way you'd get in earshot now is to *jog* and you're not about to jog up to a stranger even if you did almost get around to seeing their last movie.

Then, finally, once your brain has already become nestled in its certainty that, yes, that was Amanda Seyfried standing a few feet away from you and no, you didn't talk to her be- cause of course you didn't, what on earth would Amanda

Seyfried possibly want to hear from you? you reach the critical acceptance phase. What is so special about that person anyway? Of course they're wealthy and attractive, but they're just living their life the same way you're living yours. Their job just happens to be one that means you recognize their face and have heard them tell Jimmy Fallon about the hilarious time they went snorkeling in the Maldives. What's the big deal?

The entire journey—doubt, certainty, excitement, and finally nonchalance—normally takes place over the course of approximately twelve seconds. Any shorter than that, and you risk involuntary shrieking or ill-advised use of a cell phone camera. No, a person needs twelve seconds on average if they're going to behave like a moderate adult in the presence of a celebrity.

You had exactly a quarter of a second to register that you were inches away from Stephen Colbert on your first day of work as an intern on his television show, and you were walking up a flight of stairs, carrying a dresser.

The trouble you find with being in the first intern class of a brand-new show (at least, an old show with a new host), in a new studio, is that most of it isn't built yet. There's no order, not even the normal chaos of a television show. No one knows what cereals are supposed to go in the dispensers in the kitchen, or whether we order coffee in bulk, or if that tricycle someone sent as a joke gift is supposed to actually belong in the office somewhere. And the dressers aren't built yet.

And so when you see Stephen Colbert for the first time, he is sitting in the writer's room on the twelfth floor of the Ed Sullivan Theater talking to someone who looks very important, and you are on the stairs, directly adjacent, separated from His Royal Famousness by only a glass wall and the not-yet-built IKEA dresser still in the cardboard.

"That was Stephen Colbert in there," you stage-whisper to the intern you just met, whose name you haven't learned yet. "Right in there, that's him."

"Yeah," the intern says, straightening his glasses. "He's been in here the last few days, meeting with Brooklyn Guy. I gave his family a tour yesterday. Super nice kids." And the intern sashays away, presumably to do an important task to which he and only he was entrusted.

When you were in second grade, you had a specific fantasy that, to this day, you're not certain anyone else has ever shared. It spawned one day in the music room, when you saw the coolest girls united in a cluster on the other side of the room, all recipients of some secret code that hadn't and wouldn't be delivered to you. Why were they the coolest girls? Popularity in children is perhaps best described in the words of Supreme Court Justice Potter Stewart: "I shall not today attempt further to define the kinds of material I understand to be embraced within that shorthand description; and perhaps I could never succeed in intelligibly doing so. But I know it when I see it."

Your lack of status wasn't due to the way you dressed—your mother, keen-eyed, with three daughters, kept you more or less well stocked in whatever trend had captured the suburb that particular year—or in how you looked; there must be some aspect of your behavior, you concluded, that prevented you from ascending to the status of popular. But, if that hypothesis stood, it followed that you could alter your behavior, saying the exact right things at the right time, and then you would be popular.

Therein lay the intellectual origin of your strange, reoccurring fantasy: You didn't dream of being a pop star or a princess or of winning the lottery; you dreamed that you would be equipped with surveillance equipment—contacts you could put in your eyes with tiny cameras and a tiny microphone you could wear at all times—and somewhere, miles away, there would be an assembly of very cool people in a bunker designed for a covert military operation, and these people would watch everything you were experiencing and listen to everything happening, and they would tell you, via earpiece, what you should say and do—verbatim—if you wanted to be cool, for people to like you, for you to give off that inexplicable magnetism that some children have and some children don't, even in elementary school. You didn't even want to be the MOST popular, just part of a group of people who were comfortably established in the cool group, beyond reproach and deserving of the respect of their lessers.

The fantasy reemerged a few years later, on your first day of camp when, presented with the gift of a new social hierarchy in which no one knew you as someone whose status was middling at best, you could re-create yourself exactly as you wanted. With the maturity of a now eleven-year-old, you knew there would be no tiny cameras in contacts or microphones—you would have to operate as your own secret consultant, premeditating everything you said, and only vocalizing it if it passed your careful examination as to whether it was something a popular person would say.

You entered your cabin, buoyed with confidence in your new plan, and saw a girl, not the most popular, but popular-adjacent (how quickly these things are established with no discussion), eating her daily canteen (the afternoon treat of soda or candy), a Charleston Chew bar, while she sat on the floor. You scripted, deliberated, and then delivered your line.

"How's your canteen treatin' ya?"

She looks up at you. "What?"

It is too late to abort.

"Your canteen," you say. "How's it . . . how's it treatin' ya?"

"How's it *treating me*?" She says those two words back to you dripping in something between pity and genuine befuddlement. You mumble an apology and pretend it never happened, although, more than a decade later, you can still replay every moment of the scene—the door you entered, where she was sitting on the floor, the sinking in your stomach when you realized you said something wrong—on command.

But you are twenty-two now. And you have been told so many times to "just be yourself!" that it's more or less balanced the advice you have given yourself of "just do everything as if some spies were instructing you on how to be cool." And you have an internship at *The Late Show with Stephen Colbert*, which is very cool! By all objective metrics, you could be in that group of spies advising on coolness!

You interns are all cautious animals, deferential among your superiors (the staffers) and inquisitive about your colleagues, the other bright-eyed college kids in clothes you all bought the night before at Ann Taylor so you'd look put together for your first day, perfect straight spines and fixed smiles. *Who is going to be the champion intern?* you all wonder. Who will be the one that's promoted to full-time employee, presumably because they were the best at restocking paper towels to the sink on the third floor. But above all, the hesitation exists among the interns because there's no social hierarchy yet. You've all come from different schools and share no social overlap. Who is the coolest? Can you tell by their clothes? Or the way they introduced themselves? "Oh, I'm studying film at Tisch." Is that cool here? None of you have any way of telling, and so you're all acting extra polite to one another just in case. Everyone wants to be friends before they get to know each other.

It's nice to imagine working in television as a meritocracy, that a bright-eyed, earnest Midwesterner could make it if they were bright-eyed and earnest enough. Maybe that's true somewhere. But not here, not after the question interns ask each other after names and schools: "So how did you get this job?"

The answers vary, but they tend to have a similar thematic thread. My mom is a chief of programming. My brother-in-law works in accounting. Jon Stewart owed my dad a favor. I have photographic evidence that proves a CBS executive hit a dog and drove away, and I handed it over in exchange for an internship. The usual. There are two of you who answer with mock incredulity. "Why, I just sent in a résumé? Isn't that how everyone gets a job here?" In actuality, you were hoisted into the running by one of the two female writers who saw your jokes on the Internet and was kind enough to humor you for a few minutes while you begged her for career advice. And even then, you were likely only hired because of your previous internship on *Conan*, which you no doubt were hired for based on a fortuitous name-drop of a Brown alumnus who also happened to be the former executive producer. The game is connections, and enough money in your savings account from your bat mitzvah to make it through a few unpaid summers. You are one of a class of privileged elitists and you are alternately ashamed and wildly grateful.

"Dana, could you go up to see Amy?" the intern coordinator calls through the door of her office.

You spring to attention. "Who is Amy?" you ask one of the other interns.

"Stephen's assistant," she says, glancing back at the other interns to gauge whether making fun of your lack of knowledge is something that's more likely to win or lose points.

And so you don't ask which one is Amy's office. You find it largely by trial and error (mainly error, and then politely asking one of the production assistants).

"Oh, good," Amy says when she sees someone enter her office so bright-eyed and confused at the world that they could only be an intern. "I need you to buy Stephen a putter." She thrusts a credit card into your hand.

"What kind of putter?" you say. You can be responsible. You will not come back with the wrong thing. "I was actually a golfer in high school."

"Oh, thank God," Amy sighs. "Because I have no idea what sort of clubs are out there. This is just for putting around in his office."

"How...tall is he?" you ask. Now that you have established yourself as the golfing expert, you must protect your reputation.

"Five-eleven and just bring it back here when you have it. Thank you so much."

You could've asked a hundred more questions—does he need a cup to putt into? Does he need balls? How expensive should the putter be?—but Stephen's assistant has already returned to her work and given the unmistakable body language signal for "get going already."

You practically skip to the golf store fourteen blocks away. Your fingers never leave the edge of the credit card.

The store is closed when you arrive, two minutes away from opening. An employee is sweeping the area right in front of the door. You try to make eye contact. It's *two* minutes. Can't they just open up early? You have a job to do. "You don't understand," you fantasize about shouting through the glass. "This is very urgent. This is an errand for Stephen Colbert."

You tap your foot. You check your phone. Leisurely, as if completely oblivious to the fact that someone is waiting outside to make a purchase for a *celebrity*, the employee turns his keys and peels open the door.

"I'm looking for a putter," you declare. He gestures you upstairs.

"I'm looking for a putter," you declare to the first employee you see upstairs. "It's for my boss." Now that you're actually face-to-face with someone, it seems gauche to name-drop. "He's about five-eleven."

"Uh, okay," the golf man says. "Do you know what he's looking for in a putter?"

"Just for putting around his office."

"Oh, just grab this one, then," the golf man says, handing over a medium-sized club. "Easy."

You return to the studio heroic, with the correct putter, even if it was the only putter that was suggested to you. You enter Amy's office like a proud cat bearing a dead bird. "Oh, fantastic," she says. "Hey, Stephen, we got the putter for your office. And turns out we sent the right intern—she golfed in high school."

"No way," says a voice from the connected room that sounds very, very familiar. "Come in, putt a few with me."

This probably isn't allowed. This must be some sort of trick scenario that all new interns are faced with to see who will show proper deference and humility. "Oh no, sir," you're supposed to say, "I would never besmirch Your Famousness's putter with my putrid minimal-wage hands."

"WELL DONE!" Stephen would bellow. "Now go back and restock all of the paper towels."

But you don't, and he doesn't. You mumble something and he says, "Come on! Where are you from?"

"Chicago," you say.

"Love Chicago. Spent a lot of time there," Stephen Colbert says, setting up the ball retriever.

"I know," you say before you realize how creepy it sounds. "I'm just from the suburbs, though."

"I went to college in Evanston. Northwestern," Stephen Colbert says to you, as if you didn't already know.

"I know," you say.

Tactfully, he doesn't respond. Instead, Stephen Colbert unwraps the new putter that you didn't really have to pick out and tries it out, putting a ball and watching it roll lazily into the cup. And then he hands you the putter. "Let's see what you got."

In four years of high school golfing (I know, I know), you've been faced with shots terrifying, frustrating, and high pressure. You've teed off on a hole with a massive water hazard while both teams of coaches and a horde of parents stared at you. You've had to hit, red-faced, when you were already three strokes behind everyone else and the rest of the foursome was getting impatient. You've putted on the ninth hole where sinking the shot is the difference between winning and losing.

This putt, on carpet from three yards away, is the hardest shot you've ever faced in your life. You pray to the patron saint of interns and former high school nerds and tap the ball. And it goes in the hole.

Immediately, you hand the putter back to Stephen Colbert. You are one for one, batting a thousand; it can only go downhill from there. Besides, there's a fine line between a celebrity talk show host being polite to his intern and the intern not being able to take a hint on when they're overstaying their welcome. "Nice shot!" Stephen Colbert says.

In your entire life, you will never have a better first day of work.

Continue reading.

SO YOU MADE IT TO NEW YORK. You have a job; you have a place to stay (a friend of a friend on Facebook happened to be offering up an empty white room on the second floor of a building next door to a gas station and across the street from a gas station and a vape shop. The neighborhood could generously be called "East Williamsburg," but more accurately would be described as "No Man's Land East of Williamsburg and North of Bushwick."). Now all you need is an adult, New York City romance with someone who understands you, someone you can have picnics with in the park and attend literary salons alongside. This city is too big and too lonely to attempt to go it alone. That's what you've realized from your weeks of working as an intern, commuting back and forth on the L train, meeting friends for drinks sometimes, but in the end, returning to your now-less-empty white room, with your laptop open on your chest until ten o'clock at night, which somehow becomes two in the morning and you fall asleep to another auto-playing YouTube video of a comedian's special you've already seen four times. You never sweep the floor, and you let your little sister's powder-blue duffel gather clumps of dust under the bed. You begin buying full boxes of cereal and Twinkies and family-size bags of Popchips to bring back to your room at night to stave off boredom. Don't be lonely. Find someone.

WHO WILL YOU FALL IN LOVE WITH?

1. Young or old?

A. Young. You are Mrs. Robinson and your taste is pool boys with puka necklaces and flip-flops who uptalk so that everything they say sounds like a question.

B. Old. Cognac old. Cracked-leather-chair old. Smokes-a-pipe old. Not like grandpa old, but I mean, if he happens to have a few superyoung grandkids because he accidentally had kids as a teenager or something, that's cool.

2. Comedic or literary?

A. Comedic. Dating a funny guy is like a gypsy's curse: You will suffer through 1,000 terrible improv shows.

B. Literary. Dating a literary guy is like another gypsy's curse: You will suffer through 1,000 mediocre readings.

3. Emotional or withdrawn?

A. Emotional. Drunk girl crying in a bar bathroom and telling everyone she loves them.

B. Withdrawn. Under a Snuggie and holding a cat that is desperately trying to escape your grasp.

4. Charles Dickens or Thomas Pynchon?

A. Charles Dickens, populist hero.

B. Thomas Pynchon, recluse hero. I mean, Charles Dickens never got to be on *The Simpsons*.

5. Twitter or email?

A. Twitter. Microfiction is the new frontier.

B. Email. Did you know that the *New Yorker* only takes submissions via email now?

If you chose mostly As

Turn to page 135.

If you chose mostly Bs

Turn to page 144.

HERE, YOU THINK TO YOURSELF, IS A BOY YOU COULD DEFINITELY FALL IN LOVE WITH. He wears the same stained white T-shirt every day, switching it out only for his lucky West Ham jersey when his favorite team is playing (an event he'll commemorate with fellow Brits and a few committed anglophiles at a bar in Midtown at nine o'clock on a Saturday morning). His hair is perpetually greasy but it falls in his face like Hugh Grant's hair does. You'll wonder, later, whether you only came up with the Hugh Grant comparison because he was British and conclude: maybe. He is the opposite of the douchey Wall Street investment banker bro you've declared yourself immune to. He is friends with everyone; everyone wants him; everyone knows him; everybody has a story about him.

You'll wonder why a British accent affords so much social and sexual currency in the United States. Perhaps it's because in America we become exposed to Englishmen through their princes and their bumblingly adorable classically trained actors who seemingly all went to Oxford. You meet an English boy in America, and even though your brain says, *Underemployed, undershowered comedy writer,* your ears hear, *Secretly a prince who will fall in love with you and bring you on horseback to a fairy tale of castles and ball gowns.* And because an accent is so desirable, dating a boy with an accent will make all of your friends jealous; a by-product that makes the accent even more desirable.

One night, after watching an episode of *The Leftovers* in

his bed (or rather, a mattress on the floor), you realize something: When you're with him, you forget to cover your mouth when you laugh. With everyone else you're embarrassed about your extra inch of gum and the way your smile makes you look like an angler fish. But with him, you don't seem to care. He doesn't seem to mind how you look. He says you're hot and you almost believe him. When you're spending time with him, you feel as though you two are the only ones in Brooklyn who can see through the bullshit—you are mini-Holden Caulfields, but self-aware, like if Holden Caulfield had been able to read *Catcher in the Rye* when he turned eighteen. It's you against all the phonies. Sometimes, when you watch TV in bed together, he'll wrap his arm around you and you'll think, *This is how it's supposed to be.*

You're not dating—you've never been dating, not really. He calls you "man" and "mate" and punches your shoulder playfully and talks to you mostly about *The Leftovers* and not his hopes and dreams. But it's going to happen—you can feel it. The two of you will go to readings and open mics together. You'll binge-watch TV in bed from your laptop, making coffee in a French press, nestling in the crook of his arm that smells like him.

You'll be the kind of girl who has an Instagram with a consistent aesthetic, each picture merging seamlessly into the next like they were designed by a magazine's creative director. The pictures all feature a version of you who's bone-thin with long, naturally straight hair and a jawline as sharp as a hand razor (unlike your jawline, which sort of muffin-tops into your chin). There you are facing away from the camera, gazing out the window. There you are in round sunglasses, at a rooftop party. There you are drinking matcha tea and showing off your stick-and-poke tattoos. The version of your-self you are with him is daring and fearless and reckless and probably does drugs. She is irresistible.

But then, why does he never lean in to kiss you? Why does he only return your texts sometimes, and even then, two, three hours after you sent them?

You know the truth in the back of your mind. Those awful six words ricochet between your hemispheres like a current in an electrical storm when you open your phone again and again and see that he hasn't responded to you (or that he has responded to your lengthy diatribe about the meaning-ful differences between friendships and relationships with a "haha"): He's just not that into you.

And then, one night at the end of November, he comes to your place (or rather, the room you're renting in an apart-ment that claims it's in East Williamsburg but that everyone really knows is just North Bushwick) and tells you about the sort-of relationship he's in with another writer in Brooklyn, scratching at the plasticky floral cover on your apartment's communal kitchen table and looking up at you apologeti-cally.

You look her up on Facebook and Twitter, and she's gorgeous—long freckled limbs and shaggy blond hair and white smile with a job more interesting and more impressive than yours. Of course he's with her, you think. But then why is he always hanging out with you?

You once read an article that said, contrary to what people might expect, those with high IQs are far more likely to be seduced by a cult than those with lower IQs. The reason being that people who are more intelligent are also more cre-ative: They might be faced with a dossier of evidence telling them that the cult beliefs are nonsense, but a clever person who wants to believe something will be able to come up with imaginative justifications for themselves. A person with a high IQ can create entire reasoning systems designed to justify something that they want to believe is true. Do you understand where this is going?

Every joke Brooklyn Guy makes, every invitation to a party, every hug, every time he offers to open a beer for you, become tallies in your mental column for all of the reasons he loves you, or at least reasons he is interested enough to have sex with you. Because really, once a boy has sex with you, it's only a matter of time before he falls in love with you. Sure, he's a guy who sleeps around, but you're not like other girls. You're the heroine in the story. He'll have the best sex of his life with you and tumble back onto his mattress, bare chested and heaving, and whisper, "Wow."

You sleep together one time, when he is at your place late, talking about how he and the sort-of girlfriend (she of the long freckled limbs and blond hair) broke up or went on a break and how her boyfriend found out (she had a boyfriend, it turns out, in California) and how Brooklyn Guy and her boyfriend will never speak again (Brooklyn Guy and her boyfriend had been best friends, it turns out) and he's crying at your kitchen table at midnight and you should be thinking anything but what you're thinking, which is, *Maybe now he'll want to be with me.*

You hug him to comfort him, and he hugs you back, and you have that unspoken but obvious moment where a hug being face-to-face turns into a kiss and you go into your bedroom and peel off your clothing before he can change his mind. While he's thrusting inside you and his Hugh Grant hair is flopping in his face, you smile your gummy shameless smile and you know that even though all of the girls in Brooklyn and half of the girls in Manhattan have fallen in love with him, he's having sex with *you*. You've done it.

As soon as he comes, you can see on his face that he thinks he made a mistake. How can two people who were just physically inside one another have such different understandings of what just happened? You just had sex with Brooklyn Guy, the boy of your dreams. You just passed the first massive hurdle of your love story together. It's an easy roll downhill from here. His face is contrived thoughtfulness.

"That was a mistake," he says. "I'm only going to hurt you."

Here is the thing about assholes: They seem to believe that by outwardly declaring themselves assholes, they absolve themselves of all responsibility for subsequent assholery. "I will hurt you," a boy warns, and then hurts you, and then you're left blaming yourself because you knew what you were getting into. They act like being an asshole is like being diabetic or a professional mime. *Sorry, this is just an unchangeable fact about my life and who I am.* A boy can walk through his twenties in bulletproof armor if he tells every girl he ever sleeps with in advance that anything bad that he'll ever do is her fault.

But. You're sure that's how it is with other girls. Not with you, the girl he watches TV with in bed, who he invited to watch West Ham play football at a bar on a Saturday morning, the girl who, once he decides to date her, will become bone-thin and long-haired and tattooed and drink matcha tea.

"Just stay," you say, almost pleading. You're still naked.

He hasn't even taken off the condom yet. Why do you have to plead? You shouldn't be pleading, you know that, but it's too late now.

"I'm just too complicated right now," he says, condom peeled off at this point, already pulling on his boxers. You move onto your elbows, the international sign for "I will give you a blow job if you stay in bed with me." He acquiesces for about fifteen seconds, and then pulls away, which makes it all even worse. "I really have to go."

And so he leaves, and you go to the window and watch him, in a ripped parka with its fluffing contained by duct tape, walk through the snow, lit yellow by the gas station sign across the street, toward the subway.

You text him the next day because it's not like you're a person who's *good* at making decisions. And he responds.

What do you do?

A. Keep spending time with him. The longer you hang out, the more likely you'll get another chance to get him into bed with you. The more times you'll make him laugh, the more he'll have to grow comfortable with you, the type of comfortable where he'll realize maybe, just maybe, you'd be an okay person to call his girl-friend.

Continue reading.

B. Fuck him. Or rather, never fuck him again. It makes you angry, his indecisiveness, his self-conscious-but-oh-so-self-aware, pity-me-because-I'm-so-complicated-I-just-don't-want-to-hurt-you act. He thinks he can make women fall in love with him by acting like their boyfriend in every area of their lives except the actual being their boyfriend, and you fall for it, but it's not your fault; it's his. You will be the seductress from now on. You don't need an underemployed man-child with greasy hair who doesn't want you. You can do better.

Turn to page 144.

Things go back to the way they were: the television shows in bed together, the hanging out, the small acts of flirtation. The two of you arrive at a party together at a bar, and since you came with him, you feel entitled to jealousy when you see him flirting with a pretty girl with silver hair and a low-cut top an hour into the night. You leave without saying good-bye. Later, when you complain about him to your friends ("I mean, what *are* we?"), you'll hear the gossip, told to you with the faux-sympathy of someone who just can't wait to crush you. *God, he is such a shitbag,* they'll say. *The fact that he would make out with that girl at that party when he came with you? I mean, awful.* You don't care. You still spend time with him. You still text him first and drop everything to see him when he offers a sliver of his time. If you're cool enough, maybe he'll realize what you realized a long time ago: You two are meant to be.

Just as you begin to feel your real self creep into your interactions—dumb jokes, no makeup, actually being able to have fun—he'll tell you about another girl (not you, not the silver-haired girl) in Brooklyn that he's, well, sort of dat-ing. Mariah, her name is. He says she's special. The word lands in your stomach and splashes up bile. He also met her on Twitter, the same way he met you.

There are about twelve people in this world, it seems, the few of you who went to good schools who now work for the same freelance websites and have all the same friends. She has brown hair and lives in Brooklyn too. She's Jewish. She's you, but skinnier and she's special. She has something that makes him want her more than he ever wanted you. She is Cooler than you. You resent her without meeting her, seething when you see an article she's written or someone retweeting her pithy posts. You stack your accolades next to hers in your mind, as if you reassure yourself that you are enough. It doesn't matter, though, does it. She has him, and you don't.

But you have one more thing you can try, one strategy left before complete and utter impotence. You direct message the new girl he's dating, Mariah, waving a carefully sewn white flag: "Heyyy (the extra y's purposefully included, meant to induce a casual nonchalance), I know this might be weird with the whole Brooklyn Guy thing (how much does she know? Better just to be vague) but I feel like we have a lot in common and should be friends."

Sent.

She responds sooner than you expected.

"Yes! I'm so glad you reached out. Let's do drinks soon?"

Do you go out to drinks with her?

A. Yes. I mean, what's the worst that can happen? This isn't a horror movie where someone says, "Let's go to the old Victorian mansion that someone built, inexplicably, out in the middle of the woods in an area with no roads, power, or phone lines. What's the worst that can happen?" Obviously, in that scenario, the worst that can happen is that a vindictive nineteenth-century ghost will try to use your body for grotesque medical experiments in an ill-conceived and very contrived plot to avenge the death of his lost love. This is just drinks. You'll probably be fine.

Turn to page 159.

B. No. This won't end well. Reach out to someone from a different world. There was the girl who asked you to coffee, the one at the Columbia MFA program. She seems nice.

Turn to page 155.

**YOU ARE TOO NEW AT CELEBRITY INTERVIEWS TO BE PRO-
FESSIONAL ABOUT IT.** In fact, the only reason you took on
this interview (a freelance referral from a friend of a friend—
hey, is this something that might interest you?) is because you
Googled the subject and saw his picture: a smirking half-smile,
glasses, and very blue eyes. Exactly your type in the worst possible way.

He's an author—a real author, who writes 800-page novels on metaphysical existence and Jewish identity. He's been
written about in the *New York Times* and the *New Yorker*. He's
a Philip Roth–style author who probably gets weekly drinks
with Don DeLillo and has Thomas Pynchon's home phone
number. He teaches at an Ivy League MFA program. He reminds you of the writing professor in college who told you
that he thought you might be commercially successful, as if
the words were a curse that damned you to the Buy Two Get
One 1/2 Off table at an airport Hudson newsstand. You are
instantly attracted to him.

You take two subways and a bus to reach the bar in Red
Hook he suggested for the interview (it took two emails to
convince him to do the interview at all, plus a pledge that
you'd be very, very quick about it). The bar has soggy wood
and dim fish-themed lamps and a pinball machine in the
corner. The Philip Roth Guy is twenty-five minutes late, and
he orders rye whiskey.

Later that week, when you listen back to the interview to
transcribe it, you'll be humiliated at how fawning you sound,
what a sycophant you were, how long you talked about your-

self instead of dropping out of the way to let the interviewee speak. Listening to your voice recorded and played back at you is bad enough, but so much worse when you realized you were being super-embarrassing the entire time.

But in the moment, you thought you'd adopted a perfect persona: sexy ingénue reporter who's about to become very successful.

Twenty-five minutes into the interview, he finishes his rye and fingers the pack of cigarettes in his pocket. "Okay," he says. "I have to go back to work."

"Do you do anything but work?" Your piece is about his writing habits—he writes for ten hours a day and only takes cigarette breaks. His work has been described as "poststructural." A profile in the *Times* called him a genius.

"Sometimes I get drinks with friends. But I work most of the time."

"Are you happy?" you ask, desperate to get him to shed his curmudgeonly writer persona, trying to pick away at its edges the way you would the clear film on a kitchen appliance.

"That's a pointless question," he says.

You walk him home, but he doesn't invite you in.

You email him about it the next day. "You could have invited me in."

"You're writing about me," comes the terse and immediate response.

"So?" you type back. "It's not like it's going to change anything about the interview."

"What was I supposed to do?" he writes back (a quick corresponder). "Invite you in, throw you down, and fuck you when you're doing an article about me?"

"Yes," you write back.

He doesn't respond.

And so you finish the article and post it, which gives you another excuse to email him, to send him the link. "And now I'm finished writing about you."

The arrangements are made via email: Philip Roth Guy sends an Uber to your apartment to pick you up. He is fifteen years older than you, and you spend the entire car ride to his place texting anyone in your life that might be remotely impressed that you are about to sleep with an *actual writer*.

You arrive terrified and thrilled. He lives in a basement apartment in Red Hook with two locks on the door. He's barefoot when he invites you in, in jeans and a soft-looking gray T-shirt.

The room is all books—covering every surface, overflowing on bookshelves on every wall, in stacks around the room five feet tall. What furniture there is, aside from a desk and writing chair, is made of cinder blocks. His mattress is on the floor in the corner.

By the time you finish scanning the room, Philip Roth Guy is already sitting back at his desk, plunging his cigarette into an overflowing ashtray and lighting a new one. He doesn't offer you one but he does offer you a drink. You accept. He pours you a glass of wine and then returns to his desk, back to answering emails while you stand, hovering, a few feet away.

"Should I . . . sit or something?" you offer.

He just looks at you, blue watery eyes peering through thick glasses. "I like you standing there. Nervous. It's cute."

You are nervous. You wring your hands around the wine-glass before making your decision. You place the glass down on the only few inches of desk not covered by ashes or paper and straddle him. The moment your mouth is on his, he changes. He becomes a primal, animal thing, sucking, rough, kissing, arms, chest, creature. He tells you to strip. He's still fully clothed. He throws you—literally throws you—onto the mattress and begins to shed his jeans.

"Are you clean?" he asks, pulling out a condom.

"Yeah."

He peels the condom on and begins thrusting.

"Why should I trust you?" he growls. "Tell me you're clean."

"I'm...clean," you say.

"Why should I trust you? I have no reason to trust you. Look in my eyes. Should I trust you?"

"You should trust me," you answer.

"Why should I trust you?" he says again, but you know somehow that he's not looking for an answer.

"Is this how you imagined it?" you ask, breathless. "I mean, were you thinking about fucking me during the interview?"

"A little," he answers.

"Like how? How were you imagining fucking me?"

He's holding you down, pressing into you while you're lying on your side.

"On your side like this," he answers, and a hand coils upward like a cobra and wraps itself around your neck.

He finishes (you don't) and the two of you fall back on the matted sheets, smelling like sweat and semen.

He calls you an Uber back to your place and doesn't kiss you goodbye as you exit the double-locked front door. "Can we do this again sometime?" you say.

"I'm really busy."

Is he really busy? He's writing all the time. He is home, in his basement apartment in Red Hook with a mattress on the floor, drinking and smoking cigarettes. He is a cliché. You can see through the cliché, which means you can save him. His genius can't be sexually transmitted, but the social cachet of his genius can be. You will be his ingénue and he will be your older, handsome guide to the literary world of respect and esteem. You will go to parties with Jhumpa Lahiri and Michiko Kakutani and wear floor-length gowns while he stands next to you in a tux. "Yes, I know this year I won the Man Booker prize," he'll say with modesty, "but really, it's Dana's work that's going to change the world. She inspires me to be a better writer. I don't know if I've ever met anyone with more natural talent." The *New York Times* will come to your Upper West Side brownstone with a photographer and take pictures for the front page of the style section. The two of you will have a bloodhound named Lord Byron and a cat named Caroline Lamb.

"Just drinks," you offer. "Any night this week."

"Fine," he says.

And you're home, glowing, confident that you just met the man you're going to marry.

The next day, an email from him:

Work is hectic. Going to need a raincheck on those drinks.

You email back.

Good luck on your masterpiece. Let me know when you're free.

Philip Roth Guy:

I'm going to DC next week for work, probably won't be for a while.

A while is fine. He'll come around when he realizes how lonely he is in his apartment of overflowing ashtrays and bookcases.

At this point, you decide it's time to take your relationship to the next level: You head to the Strand bookstore near Union Square and slither through the stacks until you find a copy of his book.

As you're checking out, the clerk glances at the cover. "Oh, I heard this was good."

"Is it? Yeah, I've been dating the guy who wrote it, and I figure it's time to finally give it a read."

The clerk gives you a glance.

"I mean, I lied about having read it when we first met, and I figure now's the time to actually make good."

The clerk just gives a polite nod.

You sit in the park and try to read. The book is halfway between poetry and prose, but with very few paragraph breaks. The main character (who happens to have the same name as the author) is a writer, writing about someone with the same name as him. You understand this is supposed to be very smart commentary on something, but only get about four pages in before you're struck by the urge to text the author, who you're dating.

"How does next week look for you?"

Two minutes go by of you frantically refreshing your phone.

"Still in DC," comes the reply.

"When do you come back?"

No reply.

You know, deep down, that you've gone too far, that the rules of basic human interaction stipulate that someone who doesn't respond to your texts isn't into you, but the rules of basic human interaction also stipulate that you wouldn't sleep with someone if you weren't just the slightest bit into them. What did you do that was so egregious it would completely diminish his interest between one perfectly nice sexual encounter and the opportunity for a second?

Besides, he told you himself, he's not happy, and he's not good with women. He's a loner, and he needed you to make the first move before—maybe he just doesn't know how to act around you. You just have to keep peeling away—no, not peeling, *chiseling*—at his exterior until whatever lies beneath is revealed to you.

You email him again a few weeks later, and when he doesn't respond, you email again. You email with subject lines like, "remember me?" and no text in the body. Sometimes you email plaintive apologies that you hope come across as self-aware. He rarely responds.

A month later, you're relaying the saga to a friend. "He never rescheduled drinks. And I keep emailing him and he just stopped responding."

She's silent for a few seconds, and then says, in the soft tone usually reserved for children or people deeply involved in a cult: "Maybe you should stop emailing him."

You sputter. "I mean, he sometimes responds. It's not like—" But what's it not like? It is exactly what it's like. You're a drive to his house away from being a full-on stalker. Forget about him, try to delete the evidence of your humiliation in your "sent" email folder.

You still haven't gotten rid of his book on your shelf, but you haven't read it either.

Turn to page 152.

ARE YOU AN INTROVERT OR JUST A LAZY ASSHOLE?

1. You make plans to go out for drinks with a friend you haven't seen in a while, but when the day comes, you're feeling a little tired. What do you do?

A. Go anyway because you're an adult, and you're looking forward to chatting with your friend in a relatively quiet, one-on-one setting.

B. Text her two hours before you planned to meet that you're feeling sick and way behind on work. Spend the night in sweatpants eating an entire tub of Ben & Jerry's because you're a goddamn cliché.

2. Your friend is throwing a birthday party in Brooklyn. It will take thirty-five minutes to get there, and you'll need to transfer subways. Do you go?

A. Yes. What else are you doing on a Friday night?

B. No. You order in and spend the night in the same sweat-pants binge-watching *Penny Dreadful* on Netflix.

3. Do you need time alone to "recharge" your batteries?

A. Yes! I am an introvert.

B. I never let my batteries uncharge.

4. What's your beverage of choice?

A. Tea in an adorable mug

B. The milk you drink straight from the bowl after your eleventh bowl of cereal

5. The friend from the first question rescheduled, and the two of you are getting brunch Sunday morning. But then Sunday comes and you're very sleepy and do not want to leave your bed. What do you do?

A. Get out of bed and meet your friend because you made plans and you already canceled once.

B. Text "Pleaaaase don't hate me. I just have the worst headache and I am so behind on work. Raincheck?" and watch another episode of *Penny Dreadful*.

If you answered mostly As

You are an introvert.

Turn to page 155.

If you answered mostly Bs

You are just a lazy asshole. Be a better person. Jeez. Honor a commitment. Put on a bra *some* of the time.

Turn to page 159.

YOU SEIZE ONTO A FRIEND GROUP IN NEW YORK CITY LIKE A PARASITE ONE AFTERNOON. An acquaintance invited you to the Brooklyn Book Fair, to meet her and her friends on Saturday. "Meet there at noon?" she said. You wake up at nine and watch the clock until 10:45, when you leave your apartment in Bushwick, take a subway to Manhattan, transfer trains, and then ride the subway back into Brooklyn toward Cobble Hill. You are still a half hour early, and so you walk the stalls by yourself, savoring each one, forcing your eyes to touch every single title. You try making eye contact with boys you find cute, but most of them are either literary douche stereotypes (slouchy beanie, jean jacket heavy with buttons, cross-body bag), married, or obviously gay. A good proportion are all three.

But you're at the epicenter of the Brooklyn literary scene, and it's so warm out you find yourself drifting close enough to each tent to steal some of its shade. You buy a hardback copy of a collection from a webcomic you like, and then two paperback books you've been meaning to read, receiving a third and a free tote bag to put them all in. You sign up for every single mailing list and take every single free magnet or bookmark or cider doughnut. You are meeting a group of friends; today you have the confidence of a girl being admired. You're hyperaware of your smile and your sandals and your hair. You feel unstoppable.

"Hmm, so what's this?" you say at every booth with a flirtatious glance up at whoever's manning it. You hadn't quite anticipated spending so much time on your own, but the friends you're meeting are running late, and so you're an Independent Girl for a while longer, sashaying amongst the literary magazines and spending money on books as if your internship isn't minimum wage. And so even though you'd been hoping to save the last row of booths to visit with the group, you head there now, starting with the *Lapham's Quarterly* table.

It's hotter now than it was when you first arrived—you're keeping your arms at your side and barely concealing the sweat stains blossoming in your armpits. Your group of adoptive friends are fourteen minutes late.

There's a boy working the *Lapham's Quarterly* stand— cute, but a little young. He looks like he could still be in college. You flip through the journal's latest edition, as if you have any intention of buying it. "Ooh, I've been thinking of getting a subscription," you lie. The boy smiles and stares at your face. You feel a bit disheartened that nobody here has recognized you from the Internet. If you have any audience at all, surely it's people who work at the Brooklyn Book Fair. You have half a mind to keep flirting with the boy, just to pass the time, but just then you get a text. "We're here!!! Sorry we're late, by the Penguin bus." Penguin Random House had outfitted a van as a mobile library, with their bestsellers displayed on the outside. It's a perfect landmark to meet at. "Be right there!!!!" you text back. You put away your phone and the boy is still smiling at you when you look up.

You:

A. Smile back and head off to meet your friends amid the

crowd of people before they move and they're lost in the sea of liberal book lovers.

Continue reading.

B. Spend a little more time flirting, for fun. Just to see where it goes.

Turn to page 247.

It's easy to navigate spending time with a group of established friends when you're the guest of the week. You join in on their ribbing, don't laugh too hard at inside jokes, remember their names, and boom—you're in: a day pass to friendship. The three of you meet up with another pair and eventually there's half a dozen friends that have been absorbed, amoeba-like into a single group. You end up re-walking all of the stalls you already passed but you don't mind; you would walk past them a hundred times if it meant having company.

By four o'clock, someone declares that they're starving, and you all migrate to the Shake Shack across the street and hold down a table in the back corner. More and more people keep coming, but you are part of the original core group that reserved the table in the first place. You hold your seat like you're next to the queen at court. You are a group of comfortable strangers now, sharing your wares on the table—fries, ketchup packets, literary zines, newly purchased books—talking about ideas and jobs and writers you've never heard of.

They are all New Yorkers—either born and bred or

adopted by attending college here and instantly absorbing the city into their bones. The girls have pixie cuts and short story collections; the boys have ear piercings and ironic T-shirts. You feel a bit like a distant aunt at a family reunion, slightly out of touch with the kids. But you never once feel excluded.

You won't hang out with this group again, maybe through your own passiveness, maybe because the friendship didn't have a natural course to pursue here. You live in different neighborhoods. Even the girl you know the best, the one who invited you here, you've only hung out with once. These are people whose names you'll forget, like the friends you'll make at countless parties—fun for a few hours and then gone like cigarette smoke into the cold.

Turn to page 167.

THERE ARE FIVE OF YOU AT DRINKS THAT NIGHT, girls from assorted Internet publications wearing tight jeans and designated going-out tops, meeting at a table in the back of Art Bar in the Village like representatives from different mobster families. Three of you have slept with Brooklyn Guy and had your heart broken (the damage remaining in various degrees). And then there's Mariah, holding court as the Queen of Those Who Have Been Screwed Over by Brooklyn Guy, even though she's the only one of us who is still with him. "Ugh, I know he's the worst." (She's still dating him.) "What did we all see in him?" (She's still dating him.) "I swear, a guy with a British accent in New York can get away with anything." (She's still dating him.)

Three rounds of martinis later, you declare yourself a coven. Despite being a gang of women writers who spend too much time on the Internet always competing for the same accolades and bylines, the coven has evolved past the pettiness of women competing with women. You and Mariah are being radical empowered feminists in your ability to be friends with one another united against a fuckboy who screwed you both over like the Furies of mythology (she's still dating him).

For the first time in your life, you're introduced to the political terror that is a group chat. It's impossible to keep up with each individual thread of conversation as they whip past, notifications dinging and silenced on your phone, alerting you to the fact that other social lives are continuing without you while you're still in bed, holding your phone.

But the most important thing is that you're in the group chat. This feels like the alpha group of New York millennial girls, and for the first time in your life, you feel as though you are a qualified member.

You were sixteen when you begged and wheedled your parents into spending an unrepeatable sum of money to send you on a summer program for teenagers to Europe. You ordered a dozen brochures to be sent to your house and spent hours poring over the glossy pictures of happy friends eating gelato and contemplating beneath trip titles like "Fabulous France!" and "Ciao, Bella: The Hidden Wonders of Italy!" Eventually, you settled on a three-week program through Spain. It would be perfect, and you'd come back brilliant and fluent in Spanish, with a camera full of photos with you among your new friends for life, smiling and gleeful and ready for inclusion in next year's brochure.

Your mother had warned you, before you left, that this program was known for attracting a faster crowd, kids from New York. That's how she referred to them, "faster," meaning more grown up, quicker to drink and have sex, to learn the quick dopamine rush of cruelty, to feel confident enough to cast themselves into the struggle for popularity. She bought you a pair of black Nike sneakers to wear, the type she promised they would have, so you would fit in, and you wore them to the airport.

Your mother dropped you off with the group with a hug and a semi-tearful kiss beyond the earshot of the fast kids, reclining against their suitcases, parentless already, gazing over and evaluating you, from your Nike shoes up.

But Nikes or not, you were still the Midwestern bumpkin of the "how's that canteen treatin' ya?" variety, the only one from public school, from Chicago, the overanalytical suck-up who wanted to go to museums instead of bars and who clung to the establishing cliques of disaffected New York teenagers like a barnacle.

At every new town, the counselors—early twenties, with sunburnt noses, men and women bare shouldered in college tank tops—asked the group to submit their hotel requests, to inform them of who you wanted to share a room with. The cliques, with their courtly political strategies, had a silent and seamless rotation. You never had a request. In every city, room after room, you ended up sharing with a fellow outcast, a nearly silent girl with butt-length black hair that hung in thin, shedding strings, a girl who no doubt resented you as much as you resented her (even with her terrible hair, she was still a private school girl, from New York).

You affixed yourself desperately to one of the cliques, a trio, that seemed to tolerate your presence—you would be silent and opinionless, trading all personality for the lifeboat of their company during the free hours the program gave the group to shop and eat. Don't try to understand their jokes; accept that they'd probably just been talking about you while you were in the bathroom, ask them for pictures anyway so you'll have some to put up on Facebook and pretend like you had an amazing time.

A week before the program was to end, the trio's de facto leader pulled you aside after lunch. "We were talking, and it feels like you're just spending too much time with us. Like, just try to branch out maybe?"

You couldn't stop the tears from coming. "With *who*?" you managed to gasp out between sobs. She shrugged. The nicest member of the trio gave you a sympathetic glance. The last one avoided eye contact.

It's been a decade since that trip and you have rebuilt yourself: confident, funny, brash, unapologetic, and most importantly, surrounded by people who enjoy that kind of thing. Boys generally seemed willing to let you slink into their dorm room beds more often than not; you went to Brown, which comes with the cache of Emma Watson (who you never actually saw) and Serena van der Woodsen (who is fictional), and you have a Cool Job in New York City, an internship at *The Late Show with Stephen Colbert*, which is the type of job you can drop, subtly, at any party and bask in a tiny moment of recognition and envy. You have enough Twitter followers to exchange them for social currency. You have been told there is a New York Twitter Media Scene, and you are confident you can purchase entry.

But the gatekeeper seems to be this girl Mariah—a pot-smoking, lifelong New Yorker with bad tattoos and clinical depression that she talks about all the time. And whenever she talks, her words peel themselves from the side of her mouth with the up-talking inflection of a whining complaint. Everything she says sounds like it's behind someone's back. And Brooklyn Guy chose her over you.

You become a worse version of yourself around her—pettier, more competitive. Everyone becomes a list of their most recent publications' placements. Everyone is competing against everyone else for the same jobs and pretending like they're not.

There is only one Bond girl. There is one girl the dozen men bring along on the heist. There is one princess that entrances the male hero beyond all reason. Men can see themselves in Luke Skywalker or Han Solo or Boba Fett or Yoda or Darth Vader or Obi-Wan Kenobi. Women get the snarky princess. Men can see themselves as the Beast or Gaston or Lumiere or Cogsworth or Belle's oddball father or LeFou. Women get the snarky princess. Men can see themselves in Simba or Mufasa or Timon or Pumbaa or Scar or Rafiki or Zazu. The female option, once again, is snarky princess, only this time she's a lion. The pattern repeats endlessly. Men get champion and mentor and sidekick and comic relief and villain and advisor. Women get one impossibly gorgeous character some middle-aged man decided would be the only iteration of an empowered female.

There are exceptions, of course. Sometimes a woman will be permitted to be a mother figure—round like a baked loaf of bread, nonthreatening and unsexualized—or a whore, the street-smart girl who sacrifices herself so that the innocent heroine can be happy. But options are severely limited. If a girl wants to be an object of desire and not mockery, she has to be the one who isn't like other girls. Which is only possible if someone else hasn't already taken that slot.

Perhaps in another universe, a version of you is benevolent and level-headed. *Ah, Brooklyn Guy wasn't the boy for me!* this Bizarro-version of you would think. *I hope he and Mariah are happy—they both deserve it.*

But hanging out with Mariah is a delicious exercise in pain. She'll complain about him, *how he won't commit, how he doesn't return her texts* and then glance apologetically in your direction. "Oh, God. Sorry."

"Oh, not at all," you'll say, fantasizing about him breaking up with her and falling back into your arms. "I'm totally over him."

You'll see pictures of them in bed together, silly texts that she'll accidentally scroll through when you're around that he sent her. You wonder if she's playing her own game with you. She, the sadist, you the masochist, the boy in the center completely unaware.

And then the day comes. Mariah has fallen out of favor like we all fell out of favor; she hates him, she loves him, she talks about him. She still sometimes talks with him, you gather. Maybe he still wants her. Maybe she's still hooking up with him. Maybe she's talking about you with him, the two of them on his bed, laughing about how desperate and obvious you had been, scrolling through your tweets and making fun of them one by one. You let her cry on your shoulder. You agree that he is an asshole with greasy hair who doesn't shower enough, who just used you all.

And then, when Mariah isn't looking, you text him.

"Heard you broke up," you write. "How you feeling?"

He doesn't respond for two hours, and then when you finally see his name on the front of your phone, your heart sputters with electric charge. And then you read his message.

"This is all really fucked up," he wrote. "You're going around the city with your little club of girls telling everyone that I'm an asshole."

He's not wrong.

"Jesus. Dana. What is wrong with you? Are you trying to ruin my life?" he says. "I don't want to be a part of this anymore."

Somehow, there has to be a perfect combination of words that, like a magical spell, will bring him back to your side. There has to be a way out. There has to be something you can say that will make him realize that you only did all of that because you loved him and he didn't love you and you were just mad and jealous and desperate. Where is the committee of Cool, Popular Secret Agents who have been watching this entire time through tiny surveillance cameras who can tell you exactly what to say and do to straddle through the lasers and make it to the other side?

"Well it's true," you type. "You were an asshole. It broke my heart having to act like your friend without being with you." You exhale with the whooshing sound that means the text went through.

"I told you from the beginning I didn't want anything," comes the reply. There is ice in those words. Not just ice. Hail, sleet, rain. It's a fucking blizzard. "I don't know what sort of weird game you and Mariah are playing with your coven or whatever. Just... leave me alone."

He's right. You had built a little gang of Empowered Women! who were all screwed over by the same guy (swirl your wineglasses, roll your eyes, amirite?) only because you desperately, desperately wanted him in your life somehow. You couldn't stop talking about him, and the only people who would tolerate you when you couldn't stop talking about the boy you slept with once were the girls who also couldn't stop talking about him.

Brooklyn Guy is gone. He blocks you on Twitter, and you, in misguided vindictive fury, block his phone number.

Over the next few days, the group texts sputter into infrequency and then finally stop altogether and you realize, with a creeping awareness, that a smaller cluster of girls have formed a new group chat, without you. Your selfishness, your insecurity, your jealousy, your cruelty: It all bubbles up inside of you in a moment while you're scrolling pointlessly on your laptop one afternoon. After a few moments of inactivity, the screen goes dark, and you're left staring at the black mirror balanced on your stomach. It shows the double chin and the frizzy halo of unwashed hairs and the grimace of chapped lips and the cluster of acne around your eyebrows.

You see them in pictures on Instagram at brunches you weren't invited to. Your little coven is over. And you're left lonelier than before with a stone in your gut that ached whenever you thought about what happened, how you needed to be loved so badly that you became someone unlovable.

How do you salvage your pride and self-esteem?

A. By getting a new boyfriend immediately and forgetting all about Brooklyn Guy. But ideally, getting a new boyfriend that would make him jealous.

Turn to page 167.

B. By trying to meet another group of friends.

Turn to page 155.

WHICH SEXUAL FETISH BEST FITS YOUR ZODIAC SIGN?

Aquarius: Sex on the beach
Pisces: Water sports
Aries: Latex
Taurus: Anal
Gemini: Threesomes
Cancer: Hotel room sex
Leo: Knife play
Virgo: Exhibitionism
Libra: Being blindfolded
Scorpio: Using candle wax
Sagittarius: Teacher role-playing
Capricorn: There's something about wearing lingerie that makes you feel like Marilyn Monroe, like, you should be in a silk robe, popping bonbons into your mouth with perfectly manicured fingernails. You'd be draped seductively over satin sheets in a room that you call your "boudoir" with a seductive purr.

But you are not in some glitzy dressing room or hotel lobby

surrounded by singing men in top hats. You are exiting a cab in Bushwick, on an empty street flanked by an empty lot on one side and by warehouses on the other, wearing a corset that belongs to Suze, who is at least three sizes bigger than you in the boob area, and all of the corset tightening in the world can only do so much to help the inch or so gap that exists between the rigid, boned fabric of the corset and the top of your boobs.

"This is the address," the cabdriver says hesitantly, watching the four girls leave the back of his cab. Suze bounds out, as the de facto ring leader (i.e., the only one who knows where she's going). In addition to the corset you borrowed from her (red brocade—she's in her black leather one), you're wearing her makeup, but your own jeans. "Last time it was in a different building, but I think they change them every month just for, like, safety stuff," Suze says, scanning the buildings for an address number.

"Safety stuff?" you ask.

"Yeah, just like so the same creepers don't show up. That's why you had to register online and bring your ID."

Suddenly, you seem very far from your bed and your laptop, and a realization opens in your mind like a cracked egg. "Is this . . . an orgy?"

Suze is already bounding through a thick Frankenstein-looking door and climbing the dim staircase. "It's a make-out party," she says. You know that. That was what she'd told you, and that's what had been on the website through which you bought your ticket and offered up your name and the promise that you were over eighteen. "But, I mean, yeah," she adds when she hears your hesitation. "People will probably be having sex."

"IDs?" says the man at the door. Whatever you imagined

a bouncer at a make-out-but-possibly-sex party would look like, it wasn't this. This man is slightly overweight and appears to be about midforties, thinning hair pulled back into a ponytail. You look beyond the entranceway and see the vibe is less sex dungeon and more "dorky college a cappella group letting loose." You see three men wearing fedoras. Every instinct in your body is telling you to leave, to go home. This isn't a place for you. Your places are bookstore coffee shops, and *Harry Potter*–themed amusement parks, not warehouses with strangers who all seem to be wearing at least one embarrassing article of clothing.

But the taxi is long gone by now, and you have no idea how far into Bushwick you've ventured, and you're already here. It's an *experience*. It will be fine.

By the time you were twenty-one years old, you still had never had an orgasm. That was just around the time you started to wonder if something might be wrong with you. It wasn't as though you hadn't been having sex— you had—or that you weren't attracted to boys—you were—but just that that particular moment, the moment as depicted in books and TV shows and Katz's Delicatessen scenes just had never happened for you. There were never "waves of pleasure" or "explosions." If "you'll know it when you have it," then you had definitely never had it. There was just general wetness and a moderately pleasant feeling and then a wait for it to be all over. Boys rarely checked. If you moaned a little, they'd be content to satisfy themselves, completely convinced that they brought you to orgasmic bliss and back again.

Even touching yourself did nothing. "Just relax and find what feels good!" said encouraging commenters on blog posts where other people complained about not being able to orgasm. Porn was either anemic or filthy. So you continued on your quest and eventually the world of written erotica brought you to strange places and acts that you hadn't read about yet in *Cosmopolitan*. It was an undeniable improvement. You were definitely making progress.

Your orgasm became something of a scientific challenge. Twenty-five percent of women are unable to orgasm, a statistic online declared. You at least deserved rigorous testing before you acquiesced to being one of the unlucky few.

And so, in the pursuit of orgasm, discovering you had a fetish was something akin to discovering a new freckle or a mole on the back of your hand. You're not sure whether it's new or if it's always been there, but oh well, you think. I guess this is just a part of who I am now and I'll have to deal with it accordingly.

And then you moved to New York, and your new friend Suze—sweet, bubbly, funny Suze—mentioned how she went to dungeons in college, and that universe of things that you had only read about in incognito mode on your computer (hiding the evidence even from your recently viewed pages) became something people, real people, were allowed to participate in.

"I—me, too," you said. "I mean, not me too, I've never done that but it...turns me on." It was far more difficult than you could imagine to tell a friend, even in the logical context of a conversation, that something turns you on.

"I should set you up with someone!" Suze said. "And there's this party next Friday you should totally come to. It'll be super casual, just to give you an idea of the scene. Do you have something you can wear?"

You didn't. So you borrowed a corset. And took a cab with

her to a place filled with a subculture of people you had always assumed would never intersect with your life in any way.

The room had filled up—people were smoking on the patio, and you'd have to press up against at least a few embracing couples if you wanted to cross the room.

"Cash-only bar," Suze says. "I'm going to go to the bathroom." The other two girls you arrived with have already left to wait in line for drinks. You look at Suze. "Just...mingle," she says.

A karaoke stage and microphone languish empty and unloved in the far corner, between a few dark, black leather couches low to the ground that you already know are going to see some fluid exchanges later. There is almost no one here that you want to make out with. A few cuteish boys hover around a Spin the Bottle game that someone started, but they all seem to already have their arms around girls a little cuter and a little skinnier than you. *Why are you here if there's no one you actually want to have sex with?* you ask yourself. And then there's the more important question: *Why are these people playing Spin the Bottle like they're horny middle schoolers?*

"Meet anyone cute?" Suze asks when she returns, bearing a bottle of beer.

You shake your head. "I don't think it's really my crowd."

"Mmm, yeah." She looks around. "I think the last one had a cuter turnout. I mean, we should still try to have fun."

Suze joins the game of Spin the Bottle.

Here is what having fun looks like at a sort-of orgy for you:

You scan the room looking for someone with the least embarrassing attempt at a sexy vampire goth aesthetic (think eyeliner and fishnet gloves). You politely reject the few truly pitiful boys in Hot Topic necklaces that approach you.

BOY IN HOT TOPIC NECKLACE: So where are you from?

YOU: Chicago

BIHTN: Cool. Want to make out?

YOU: No, thank you.

BIHTN: *walks away*

It's an easy and loyally-held-to formula.

You can join the game of Spin the Bottle or step outside onto the patio, where the couples who have moved very quickly past making out have decided is a good spot to claim and sprawl across the lawn chairs in a mosaic of unidentifiable ass cheeks. Instead, you watch Suze drift from group to group, occasionally joining mouths with a boy or girl of relative attractiveness. You're here, so...

"Hey," you say to a boy who is not cute, but is tall, and sometimes those can be the same thing. "Want to make out?"

He shrugs and puts his arms around you and you kiss for a few minutes—strange, not unenjoyable minutes. And then you two separate, and ten minutes later you see him kissing another girl, because that's what this place is. You just got your feelings hurt by a stranger at a party designed for people to kiss a bunch of people.

The line at the bar hasn't diminished and so you're facing down the rest of the night sober.

Why does everyone who is into BDSM also have to be into The Nightmare Before Christmas? you think as a girl walks by with Jack-Skellington patterned leggings disappearing into combat boots. What is it about enjoying a little spanking in bed that also coincides with Tim Burton's aesthetic?

You are on the island of misfit toys in cheap pinstripe tril-bies. The white-collar sadist types have to be out there, most likely snorting cocaine somewhere in Murray Hill by the thousands, but you are hardly the lithe girl in Tiffany earrings who marries a Wall Street broker. Who is left for those of you (hopefully) destined to date non-sociopaths?

Once, you and your little sister convinced your parents to take you to the Bristol Renaissance Faire in Wisconsin. It had been advertised with a big sign on the interstate, and the four of you drove gleefully, imagining giant turkey legs and a few bitter teenage employees furtively texting from phones hidden in jester uniforms, maybe a few horses trotting around a dusty field.

Instead, you paid for your tickets and entered a small nation-state. The faire was massive and sprawling, multiple "realms" with full rides and endless booths selling clothing, weapons, and vaguely medieval-themed accessories. "Look at this," your mom said, calling you over to a booth selling armor. She held up a chain-mail shirt. "Four hundred dollars."

"It's all crafted by hand," the booth vender offered helpfully.

"I just can't imagine who is investing all of this money to come here," my mom said. "Do they come week after week?"

"They must," I replied, watching a woman with an overflowing corset pass on the arm of a man cosplaying Criss Angel. "It's like a community, right? It has to be. You invest in the costume and come to the faire. It's a hobby."

It felt like we had been permitted a secret glimpse into a strange and extensive club that was at once both completely foreign and far more massive than we could have imagined.

It's the same with this party. A part of you wishes you could say fuck it all and throw yourself into this society of guys in eyeliner and girls who wear fishnet tights, people who do exactly what feels sexy to them and damn to hell anyone who might shame it in the outside world. But a bigger part of you just wants to go home.

Suze is still off playing Spin the Bottle, flanked by the other friends you came with. The black couches in the back of the room are, as you predicted, now writhing with bodies. It's time for you to leave.

You say goodbye, walk down the narrow stairs to the street, and find a corner where mercifully a cab appears as if summoned by your desperation and the universe's recognition that a girl should not be outside in Bushwick, alone, wearing a corset and coming out of a sex party.

You've tasted the BDSM world for the first time. Do you continue?

A. Yes. Try to meet someone. See if it works for you in real life.

Turn to page 175.

B. No. Revert back to the version of yourself at the last save point. This will never be for you.

Turn to page 226.

SUZE DOES END UP INTRODUCING YOU TO SOMEONE, a man she has been hooking up with. "He's nice, and safe, and you'll have fun with him," she says. She's right. Things have been going well.

Before your third date, he sends you a text. "My place, 8pm. 76 B——St. Bring gym shoes."

You've never gone out with a dominant man before, someone who would actually call himself a "dom" because he's involved enough in the BDSM scene to know what that even means. Two months ago, you barely knew there *was* a BDSM scene outside of middle-aged swingers in Akron and dungeons for senators getting whipped by high-class call girls, but it feels very New York to have a BDSM lawyer for a boyfriend—like Christian Grey or Patrick Bateman. Preferably the former because you've been wearing your nice Big Girl coat that your mom bought you from Banana Republic over to his place and you don't know how to get bloodstains out of wool.

"I don't really form attachments with people easily," he said to you on your first date. You went to a crepe place on the Lower East Side, arriving five minutes early so you had to linger in the tiny restaurant, eyeing the other tables and hoping you didn't look too much like a lost tourist with your backpack on.

The only photograph you had of him was a bruised ass from his FetLife profile. He could be anyone.

Then a man came out of the back of the restaurant, the restroom, wearing a full suit, and you didn't really think it was him, until he made his way over to you and kissed you on the cheek.

He was older than you expected, with a receding hairline like a golf sand trap and sleepy eyes that reminded you of Matt McGorry from *Orange Is the New Black*. He recognized you more easily than you would have liked; you'd strategically placed a black bar over the eyes on your FetLife profile that Suze had built with you and forwarded over to him (a comparatively mild picture of you leaning seductively over your friend's couch in a black robe with cascading cleavage).

"That easy to recognize me?" you asked.

"Yup," he answered simply, and took a sip of water. So he wasn't one to "yes and." But that's okay. Maybe you'd been dating too many freelance writers who had nothing better to do than spend their parents' money on UCB classes. He was an adult. With a job. And a suit. He paid for a cab back to his place.

He doesn't tell you what the gym shoes are for—you secretly hope it's a strange sex thing and not going to the gym together, because you hate running the way a girl who grows up the slowest one in her class will always hate running. You go to a gym exactly three times a year when enough motivation accumulates in some forgotten region of your brain that you are forced to buy a new pair of expensive headphones and an app on your phone that promises to train you for a 5k because *this time* you're going to be one of those girls who works out, goddammit, this time it's going to stick! (It doesn't.)

"Should I eat dinner before?" you text back. You're hoping that your very subtle hint will remind him that 8:00 p.m. is what you consider on the late end for dinner and you get hungry, especially when your meal will only come after a mystery sex or exercise adventure.

"No, but a snack or something is fine," comes the reply.

As of now, here are the possibilities of his mysterious gym shoe requirement ranked in order of how much you'd enjoy them:

1. He's taking you rock climbing at an indoor climbing wall-slash-restaurant. The benefit of this option is mostly food.

2. He's taking you rock climbing at a normal indoor climbing wall. The downside here, obviously, is no food. Another downside is he will see how little upper arm strength you have.

3. The gym shoes are for a sex thing. (Your lack of upper arm strength might also come into play here?)

4. He's going to make you go to the gym with him.

At 7:58 you show up at his thirty-eighth-floor apartment, wearing the jeans and sweater you wore to work that day but presciently packing exercise clothes just in case in your backpack alongside your gym shoes.

The Lawyer opens the door and wraps you in his arms with an exaggerated smack of a kiss, almost lifting you off your feet, which makes you acutely aware of all 156 of your pounds. "You bring gym clothes?" he confirms.

You lift your backpack. "So that's what we're doing?" you ask, all innocence.

"Yeah," he says, already unbuttoning his shirt and walking into the bedroom to put on a T-shirt he can sweat in. "It's been like three days since I worked out and I needed to work out tonight but I wanted to see you."

Are you flattered or insulted? Is both a valid option?

Going on a date to the gym is not something you can brag
to your friends about, but it is something you feel like
Couples do. The type of couple that you never imagined
yourself being a part of. You always envisioned yourself in
more of a *Doctor-Who*-and-microwave-popcorn couple, not
a   bouncing-ponytail-and-matching-track-jackets-jogging-
in-the-park-together-and-looking-like-Norse-gods-which-
is-how-all-joggers-look-to-you couple.

**It's 8:15 now and you're starving. He wipes his nose
and pulls his headphones around his neck, looking at
you expectantly. What do you do?**

A. Kiss him. Hard. Pull off his shirt. Pull off your shirt. Take
    him to bed and try your hardest to make him forget
    about the exercise plan.

Go to page 179.

B. Change into your shorts, sports bra, and strategically sexy
    tank top. You are Game. You can be that girl who goes
    to the gym with her boyfriend.

Go to page 180.

THE LAWYER LEANS INTO THE KISS FOR A FEW SECONDS AND THEN PULLS AWAY. "Ah, ah, ah," he says. "After." And he rolls his eyes. You've never seen a thirty-year old man roll his eyes before. "Get dressed," he says. The shadow of his pecs are visible through his T-shirt that broadcasts his mediocre law school. "Don't worry, it won't be a super tough workout."

Turn to page 180.

"YOU WANT TO DO IT ON AN INCLINE, SEE?" the Lawyer says, leaning over from his treadmill where he was running with heaving strides and punching up the incline so your treadmill shudders and lifts its head like a curious animal. You want to be an easygoing girl, a cool girl, God forbid you're "high maintenance," so you pretend as if running is something you do all the time and not the three times a year that you think, "Hey, do you know what would be fun? Almost puking."

You concentrate on your strides instead of how your hair is probably frizzing into a halo and stare at the LED clock on the treadmill, counting by the seconds. On one hand, this is a very bad date. This is the date equivalent of taking someone to the Laundromat because you needed to do some laundry. But, on the other hand, maybe it's a sign that he sees you as a possible partner, and not one of a harem of sex partners in his polyamorous life, added to the rotation as a favor to your mutual friend Suze.

Him being polyamorous doesn't bother you, not really. When he's with you, he's affectionate and interesting; he pulls up old B-horror movies on TV that he thinks you'll like and watches your face during the exciting parts to make sure you're fully enjoying them, and he carries you, like a bride across a threshold, when he takes you to bed. Besides, he's an adult with an apartment that has a doorman, a wall of windows, and a table shaped like Westeros from *Game of Thrones* that he made himself. He has a respectable job and a cute smile with dimples—if finding a good man in New

York is as hard as *Sex and the City* has led you to believe, he's a catch, even though he's probably having sex with other girls.

You know couples who are in open relationships—who have their primary partners and then ask permission to hook up with ego-boosting strangers on the side. Sometimes it feels like *everyone* you know is in an open relationship. Maybe it's the modern way to do it when you're young and in love and fully trust one another. Maybe it's the only way to do it, and the resistance you have is just you being selfish and possessive and jealous.

It's been fourteen minutes on the treadmill and your heart is four pumps away from exploding. You begin a trotting walk. "I'm...going...to...head back upstairs," you get out between dry heaves. He looks at you like a disappointed parent and rolls his eyes (again).

"It's fine," you say quickly before he can get a word in. "I'll just go back to your place and hang out."

"I'm probably not going to be done for a little while," he says, not looking over at you.

"That's fine. Where are your keys?"

You catch your breath in the elevator back up to his apartment and you realize (1) wow, you should really get in shape; that was harder than it should have been, and (2) you are starving.

Upon examination, his fridge contains two containers of Fage Total 0% Greek yogurt, a slab of raw meat, a bundle of asparagus, and four cans of Coke Zero.

You contemplate ordering Seamless but you remember as you sit on his couch and crack open your computer that you haven't gotten his Wi-Fi password yet. So you peel the tab open on a can of Coke and sit on the couch, pressing buttons until *Say Yes to the Dress* comes up on his enormous television, refreshing Twitter on your phone. You pull a book from his shelf (*Neverwhere* by Neil Gaiman) so when he comes in, you can be reading—the perfect image of the shy intellectual love interest. *See?* the book will say. *I'm more of a reading type than a working-on-the-treadmill type.*

You jump when you hear the door clatter open even though you haven't been doing anything wrong (you don't have time to snatch the book onto your lap). "You here, babe?" he calls. He's panting, and so covered in sweat he might have been swimming. The sweat stains bloom in Rorschach stains across his T-shirt. You see a butterfly and a guillotine.

"You didn't shower," he says, using the bottom of his shirt to wipe the sweat off his forehead and flash a truly wonderful strip of abdominal muscles.

"Oh. I didn't want to not hear you knocking if you needed to be let in. I had your key."

He smirks. "The door was unlocked."

"Oh. Yeah. Sorry."

You're not sure exactly what you're apologizing for, but you want him to like you. And that seems to mean playing the deferential guest in whatever way fits best against his rough edges without friction.

"You hungry?" he asks, opening the fridge.

"YES."

"Sit your pretty little ass back down, then. I'm making us dinner."

He pulls out the raw meat and the asparagus and a large stick of butter, and half an hour later you are eating steak with a boy, the first boy who's ever cooked you a meal. And it's very, very good—asparagus crisp, butter dripping down the steak. Cooking this dinner feels like something a boyfriend would do for you, even if there are no carbs.

When he takes you to bed that night, he starts by restraining you with the Velcro straps that are attached to his bed, under the mattress, and then he leaves the room, forcing you to writhe to try to see where he went and to get into a comfortable position. You had never been tied up in bed before you met him.

The Lawyer returns brandishing a long, thin knife (knives are always brandished), and he straddles you, knife casually tracing the surface of your skin.

"This is one of your carotid arteries," he says, pressing the knife's tip just a little too hard into your neck, "which brings blood to your brain. I could stab you right here." He raises the knife slightly. Of course, this is all just part of his game; this is just the sex thing he's into. Suze would never set you up with a murderer; he has to be perfectly safe. But what if he isn't? You're tied up, a man much stronger than you is above you, and he's holding a knife. Maybe he gets off on torturing girls. Maybe this is how you die. But of course it isn't. It can't be.

"One slit and you're gone," he whispers. The knife returns, softly, to your skin and it continues its route across your collarbone, down your chest, around one breast. "I could hack off a breast," he says. "Or just a nipple. Would you do that for me? Let me cut off a nipple?"

Before you can answer, he drowns you in kisses. "No, no, no," he coos. "I would never. I would never. But I don't even need a knife, do I?" To demonstrate his point, he drops the knife off the bed, where it lands on the carpeting with a soft *ting*. He rubs the left side of your lower stomach. "These are your kidneys, right here. If I punch hard enough, it would hurt more than anything you've ever experienced." He lifts a fist with a sharp inhale of breath and you wince and try to pull away. The punch comes, but not with much force. "No, no, no," the Lawyer says. "I would never."

The games last another hour before the sex happens the way sex always happens—thrusting, increasingly sweaty thrusting, pretending it doesn't hurt when it goes too deep, moaning so he thinks you come—and then he flops down on the bed next to you, depleted. You didn't come. For all of the foreplay and excitement, all of the novelty and props, you never physically got any farther than just simply being turned on. It's your fault, presumably. You just take too long. Here is a boy bringing out an entire circus of BDSM party tricks and the most your miserable body can provide in response is, "Cool. Not bad."

But you have never been able to orgasm from a man's attempts, either frantic or lazy. Orgasms are reserved, it seems, for those moments you open incognito mode on your computer and find some shameful porn that becomes more shameful the moment you finish. You watch things similar to what the Lawyer does to you and says to you. Why is it so much hotter when it's happening to someone else? There is literally nothing you can think to ask for in bed that would help you finish. A boy's mouth always feels wet and tickling, never pleasurable, and always eclipsed with the self-consciousness of *Oh God, how long is he going to want to do this, he can't really enjoy this, he's probably resenting me right now, how bad does it taste down there, I can't believe*

I didn't get a Brazilian. The only scenario you could imagine requesting that might actually work would go something like this: "You wouldn't mind me closing my eyes and touching myself while thinking about something else and pretending you're not here, right?"

It's one in the morning. You shuffle to the bathroom and rinse off in his shower, and by the time you're back, he's gone, already half dressed, in the living room on his computer. "I'm going to go to sleep," you say.

"Sure," he says. "I'm just finishing some things up."

You wake up in his bed a few hours later. It can't be morning. The lights of the city are still dim, and the sky is a smoky gray. A lamp you left on still burns orange on top of his dresser. He's still not in bed with you.

You slink through his house in the dark. You don't remember where in the apartment you left your phone and so you're walking gingerly, arms out in front of you like a mummy, guided only by the flashes of sound coming from the living room. The lights are all off, but the television is aglow with flashing lights and low-pitch noise. The Lawyer is asleep on his couch, a blanket pulled over his legs. You kiss him on the cheek.

"You fell asleep on the couch," you say, trying to sound like a sweet, long-term girlfriend. "Want to come to bed, baby?"

He murmurs and you're not sure if he hears you.

You try again. "Wanna come to bed?"

"Mmm-hmm," he mutters, and because good girlfriends aren't nags and aren't difficult and don't just tell people that sometimes they need to be held, you go back to bed and fall asleep in the big bed, alone, for the rest of the night.

Turn to page 186.

YOU AND THE LAWYER ARE TAKING A TRIP TO HOME DE-POT FOR WOOD SO HE CAN BUILD A BOOKSHELF. Yes, you are dating a boy in New York City who has a job as a lawyer, a doorman apartment, and a six-pack, and he builds furniture. He is a walking pro list. On the subway to where he keeps his car, he wraps his arms around you and kisses your face. The two of you are talking about trips.

"I'm so jealous of everyone on my Facebook feed going to Harry Potter World in Orlando," you say. The subway rattles and he tightens his arm around you.

"You want to go down there, take a trip to Disney World?" he says. "We should do that sometime."

"Really?" you ask.

"Yeah, it would be fun."

You hope other people on the subway are looking at the two of you, because you probably look so in love, like a couple that has it all figured out. (Eventually it will be these moments— the promises of trips, the home-cooked dinners, the sex that at least isn't boring—that you replay in your head when you begin questioning whether you should be with him.)

When the two of you are in the Home Depot parking lot, he turns and says, "I think you're the smartest girl I've ever dated."

"Really?"

"Yeah. Don't think I'm not impressed. The Ivy League, the perfect ACT score—it's impressive."

"Thank you," you say, and it suddenly occurs to you for the first time that he makes a list of your attributes too.

You become a stereotype of a girlfriend, bored and ornery, while he's patrolling the wood aisles of Home Depot with the energy of a caffeinated drill sergeant. As he deliberates between oak and spruce pine, comparing their relative weight and price, examining each board for knots, you feel yourself slip into what the kink community calls "a brat"—a submissive, but a submissive who acts like a needy little girl, disobeying orders and demanding attention. It's a different flavor of BDSM relationship, and it doesn't suit you. You've been aiming for "take no shit outspoken partner, half of an equal couple" but you keep sliding into "petulant child." But maybe this is what being in a relationship is? After all, you like when he takes control, when he holds you down, when he picks you up and presses you against the wall, how manly it is that he's picking out wood to make his own furniture. It turns you on, even as it makes you cringe outside the bedroom. Maybe you're a bad feminist.

The Lawyer manages to fit the planks he'll use for the bookshelf in the car by angling them from the floor of the backseat up through the gap between the two of you, a thin, red oak divider. You look out the window to help him back out.

"Have I brought you to the family business yet?" he asks, pulling out.

As it turns out, the Lawyer comes from money. His highrise apartment is thanks not to his middling legal career but to a company started by his great-grandfather, which makes caskets. He drives you deep into Brooklyn, until the buildings transform from high-rises and brownstones into squat warehouses with nondescript exteriors. You wait in the car while he unlocks the door to one of the buildings and enters.

Moments later, a garage peels open and he reenters the car to pull inside. "So are you ready for the grand tour?"

Which room of an after-hours casket company owned by the family of a guy that you may or may not be dating would you want to see more?

A. Warehouse

Turn to page 189.

B. Showroom

Turn to page 192.

THE ROOM IS THE SIZE OF AN AIRPORT HANGAR, filled with wood and the smell of sawdust. It reminds you of the massive government storage center in *Raiders of the Lost Ark*, if Indiana Jones had been in the business of protecting artifacts from Nazis that all happened to be empty, unvarnished coffins. You aren't sure whether you're allowed to touch the wood, but you can't help yourself—you run your fingers along the rough edges of the unfinished planks and rap your knuckles against their sides. It's less spooky than you would've thought upon initially hearing the phrase "casket factory." The panels of wood might as well be for building tables. There is no inkling of the future association with corpses, with decay, with loss, in this fluorescent cave with high ceilings and tight paths between the stacks of inert wood.

Toward the front of the room, there are a few assembled coffins, still just skeletal boxes with wooden sides and a wooden roof, with none of the silk or varnish that will be added later when it's wheeled out to the showroom. "You want to get in?" the Lawyer asks.

You remind yourself that you are Cool Girl. Cool Girl is always game. Cool Girl is not afraid of anything, especially not afraid of a harmless wooden box. It's a cool story, a macabre adventure out of a Tim Burton romantic comedy. Winona Ryder would totally go into the coffin. She would be super into it. You raise an eyebrow, give him a sexy sideways smile, and step gingerly inside the coffin like it's a tiny, bobbing boat, trying to keep the wheels beneath it from sliding away.

You lie down and jokingly cross your arms over your chest like a mummy or a cartoon vampire. You grin and close your eyes. He slides the coffin's heavy wooden cover back on.

You know he wants you to scream. It's the same thing he wanted when he dragged that knife across your skin. He wants you scared. But you're not claustrophobic—it's really not as bad in there are you would have guessed. Dark, yes, and quiet, but if you close your eyes, you could be lying down anywhere. You hear a creak and you know he's putting pressure on the top of the coffin so you won't be able to push yourself out. You wonder if he's getting impatient, waiting for you to beg to be let out so he can refuse you. You rustle a little inside as a compromise, bringing your arms down to your sides so you can feel exactly how confining your situation is. You can extend your elbows out about as far as you'd be able to in the middle seat of an airplane. You keep your eyes shut.

When you press against the coffin top, it's because you're more bored than afraid. You're done being alone and ready to be his girlfriend again. You manage to get it a quarter of an inch up before it falls back down onto the coffin with a hefty thud, and you're not sure if it's because the wood is heavy or because the Lawyer is still pressing on it. He hasn't spoken this entire time and you wonder offhandedly if he left you alone in there. That scares you more than being in a coffin.

"Okay, okay, let me out," you say.

There's no response.

You push once more against the coffin roof, hard as you can, but this time it doesn't move at all.

There's a heavy, rumbling thud on top, inches from your face. Something heavy is on top of the cover.

"All right," the Lawyer's voice comes, muffled. "See you Monday." You hear footsteps.

Of course he's teasing you. He wants you to be afraid. You're faking it when you say, "Come on, let me out, please!" which makes it more infuriating when he doesn't.

You try a few more moments of silence, but nothing happens. Either the Lawyer is far more patient than you are, or he's checking his phone, or he's actually walked away.

"Let me out."

No reply.

"Please."

No reply.

"Come on, please, really let me out."

"Oh, all right, all right," the Lawyer says, and pulls the cover of the coffin away and leaves you looking up at a crack of fluorescent light, the roof of the warehouse, and his face. He extends a hand and helps to pull you out. You wonder if you played the part correctly because it doesn't seem like either of you had fun.

Where to next on this date as you slowly realize this isn't going to be one of those dates where he takes you to, you know, a movie or dinner or something?

A. Showroom

Turn to page 192.

B. The Lawyer's private workshop

Turn to page 195.

IT'S ALL CHINTZ AND FLORAL WALLPAPER, like you've wandered into the home of Wes Anderson's tacky grand-mother, with plush, oatmeal-colored carpeting and bunting in pastel pink and mint green lining the walls of the show-room filled with half a dozen glossy, lacquered coffins, posed with their lids invitingly open and revealing puffed, silky pink interiors.

"Cool," you say, running your eyes down the shape of each coffin and its accompanying price, one by one. You tell yourself you are only imagining the smell of dust and formaldehyde. You are used to death and the macabre. Both are part of a sexy BDSM aesthetic—a world of corsets and men in black eyeliner and Neil Gaiman stories—but not this sanitized, pastel iteration of death that lands on your tongue like wax and hard candies from the bottom of a drawer. You and the Lawyer aren't holding hands while you pace in a small circle in the tight room, politely examining his family's wares, feet sinking deeper into the carpet with every step.

He seems completely unfazed by the morbid pastel sur-roundings. "Hey, you're writing books and things, right?" he asks suddenly.

"Yeah," you say. "I mean, I'm trying to."

"I've told you about the book I've been meaning to write, right?"

Plenty of people have told you the book ideas they've been meaning to write since "writer" became more or less your official title, but none of them have been your boyfriend.

"No," you say, as cautious as a stray dog approaching a stranger's handful of food. "I don't think you have."

He begins immediately. "So, it's like *Eat Pray Love*, right? But it's about how I got my shit together. I used to be heavy. But I started running, got into the BDSM scene—and so it's called *Work, Run, Fuck*."

He beams.

"So," you offer, "it's like a memoir."

"Yeah, a memoir and a self-help guide thing."

You swallow once. "I think something like that already exists, a parody of *Eat Pray Love*. I've seen it: *Drink, Play, Fuck*, maybe?"

The Lawyer is unfazed. "Yeah, but it wouldn't be the *same* as mine," he says, as if speaking to a child.

You sense a tiny knot of resentment coiling up inside him and sift through your mental rolodex, searching for *R*, for Right Thing to Say. "Yeah, no, you're totally right. Yours sounds really, really funny. I can't wait to read it."

"Come on," he says, not entirely convinced. "I'll take you upstairs to the apartment."

You follow him through the showroom, into a side annex with a narrow set of stairs that lead above the warehouse, opening into a small kitchen with an attached living room. The structure of it—an apartment hidden above the storage area, behind the front offices—reminds you of the tour you took of Anne Frank's house in Amsterdam.

But the apartment is—there is no other word for it— gentile. You have never been in a less Jewish series of rooms in your entire life. A dimpled white fridge, hidden beneath old school photos and postcards with Bible verses, occupies most of the kitchen. The wallpaper is pink and floral. There's a square television set sitting on the floor of the living room, and beside it a small glass cabinet, its thin legs pressing divots into the carpeting. You go closer and see the cabinet is a museum of religious curios: a cross, a Bible, dozens of tiny porcelain angels, and a tiny plastic jug of holy water, helpfully labeled.

"This is the most gentile place I have ever been inside in my entire life," you say.

"I don't know what you mean," the Lawyer replies, and the conversation ends, but you, the fun girlfriend, the teasing girlfriend, don't realize.

"Like this," you say as you enter his old bedroom. "No Jewish person has these little figurines on their dresser. Or that type of skirt on the bed."

"Those were my grandmother's. She's super religious. This used to be her room—I just stayed in it after I graduated from college before I moved to the Brooklyn place."

"I guess I can't really explain it," you say.

You stand in the pastel rooms, an island in an endless sea of draped fabric, for a few more minutes, trying to imagine ever coming back here and meeting members of his religious Italian family and not being able to.

"Come on," the Lawyer says finally. "We should head downstairs."

Continue reading.

ASIDE FROM THE WOOD-SHOP CLASS'S BASEMENT LAIR IN MIDDLE SCHOOL, you have never been in a place like this before: wide, low tables; scattered wood boards; opened cans of bubbling varnish. The walls are rough and unfinished, the door a sliding, dead-bolted thing.

The Lawyer doesn't tell you where to put your things before he strides in to examine the coloring on a bookshelf in progress and so you shrug your coat and backpack off and leave them in a corner near a wooden, horizontal X, like a multiplication sign, flat and on wheels, about six inches off the ground. You think it could be the base of something to come. This is a place of things in progress.

You head over to the worktable and watch as the Lawyer methodically dips his brush in varnish, flattens the bristles along the side of the can, and sweeps it across the top of the bookshelf.

"I'm going to put it in the entranceway, right by the door," he says. "This is just the start. I'm thinking I'll do bookshelves all the way down the hall."

He didn't ask you, but you agree with him. It would look good. "I need a bookshelf," you say. "In my new place." You just signed a lease with a friend from college on a first-floor apartment on the Upper West Side, an adult-step away from the current place you're living: that East Williamsburg place, a month-by-month rental of a room in a boardinghouse of people vaguely related to the comedy industry. You've spent the last week browsing decorating blogs, fantasizing about the room you'll have that will manage to be both driftwood-and-candles-boho and luxe-makeup-counter-chic, done exclusively with items from IKEA. As of now, you have a mattress on the metal frame it came with, two boxes of clothes, a box of books, a roll of toilet paper the previous tenants left in the bathroom, and nothing else.

"I'll make you one," he says. "As soon as I finish these."

And like that, your imaginary room gets exponentially better, because now every time someone walks in, you get to say, "Do you see the bookshelf? My boyfriend made it for me." You rehearse the tone in your head, a way that makes it sound totally casual, as if a boyfriend in New York who makes you furniture is commonplace, but also a little beleaguered, as if you *asked* him not to, but he just loves you so much he just had to make you something for your new room.

"Really?" you ask. "You... You'll really make me a bookshelf?"

"Yeah," the Lawyer says, focused on grinding at a particularly difficult patch with a scrap of sandpaper. "Why not?"

He is your Aiden from *Sex and the City*, the lovable furniture designer with a dog who proposes to Carrie and wraps her, tiny as a baby bird, in his big arms. Except he's also your Mr. Big, because he lives on the thirty-eighth floor of a building with a doorman and he always pays. And he calls you hot and talks in a cute Brooklyn accent and does strange things to you in bed in a tacit promise that the two of you will never become one of those boring suburban couples who have vanilla sex once a month and slowly grow to resent each other, him resenting her because she doesn't want it enough and her resenting him because he wants it too often, neither realizing the problem is that it's just not good enough in the first place to be able to account for a reasonable quantity.

And, most important, he likes you. He carries you to bed and responds to your texts and offers you bookshelves and trips to Disney World. You have been in New York for only four months, but you've already done it: found a boyfriend. You can check it off your list and let your single friends moan about their mediocre Tinder dates on your couch while you pour them glasses of white wine and admire your bookshelf that your boyfriend built, drove over from his Brooklyn workshop to your place in Manhattan because he has a truck, and installed himself.

"Hey," you say. "They say the snow is going to come down all night." You've already gotten a text alert from the Weather Channel and a dozen text alerts from your mother in Chicago, begging you to pick up bottled water and soup from the store before the blizzard hits full force. "How about you and I spend the entire day tomorrow in our pajamas marathoning Miyazaki movies? You haven't seen *Howl's Moving Castle*, right? It's underrated. Maybe the best one. We have to start there." You can already imagine yourself curled into the crook of his arm, under a blanket on his couch, confessing how attractive you find the long-haired, metrosexual, prickly Howl, while you watch the snow tumble from the gray skies outside his floor-to-ceiling windows.

"Ah, sorry, I have plans with a friend," he says.

"But," you say, "there's like, a massive blizzard coming."

"I know," he replies. "I haven't seen her in forever and we've had these plans for weeks. It'll be fine. I have a truck."

The couch and the blanket and the animated movies melt away like snow in summer.

"Your friend is a girl?"

The Lawyer measures the angle of a piece of wood and fiddles with it slightly. "Yeah."

"Like, a girl you hook up with?" You keep your voice as measured as you can. Don't sound jealous. Don't sound jealous. Don't sound jealous. You're Kate Hudson. Don't become the naggy, shrill brunette girl from the beginning of the movie that the audience hates and resents and will cheer when she ends up alone. He's allowed to have female friends.

"No," he spits. "I don't 'hook up with her.'" And he goes back to the bookshelf he's working on in a way that makes it clear the conversation is supposed to be over.

But you are somehow both numb and on fire and you refuse to let the conversation end here even if you know, you *know*, even before you say anything, that anything you say is going to make things worse. Twist the knife, even if the knife is inside your own stomach.

"Is it a girl you used to hook up with?"

The Lawyer looks at you, and you don't know if the look is anger or pity, but his voice is completely neutral when he says, "Yeah, I did."

"Are you going to hook up with her tomorrow?"

He puts down the brush he's just dipped in varnish. "Dana, you know what this is. You know I'm polyamorous and this was never going to be exclusive. But no," he says with a sigh, as if he's offering you the greatest concession in the world, lowering himself down to your level of crazy just this once. "I'm not going to hook up with her tomorrow. She's just my friend. But it doesn't matter."

"It's just—" You stop because you aren't sure how you want to finish the sentence. You're okay with him being polyamorous, you always were, as long as you felt like his primary partner, his girlfriend, the one he comes home to and tells about the other people, if not to ask your permission then just because the two of you are always on the same page and share everything with each other. You don't care if he gets his dick sucked by every girl in Williamsburg as long as you know that he loves you the most, that you're the one he holds when there's a blizzard outside and there's no way to leave the apartment and the two of you get to play cards by candlelight and watch movies on your laptop and fuck at two in the afternoon and then make mac and cheese on the stove because it's the only thing you have in your cabinet and you forgot to grocery shop. His friend is getting that day tomorrow.

"I just wanted to spend the blizzard with you," you say finally.

He looks at you with such tenderness and mercy that for a moment you feel ashamed of accusing him of abandonment, even in your mind. "We still have tonight," he says, and envelops you in his big arms like they're the covers on your bed and you are a child hiding from the monster that only exists if you forget to close your closet door all the way. A hand drifts down your back and lands with a spank on your ass. "Let's go back to my place."

There's already at least six inches of snow on the ground as the two of you trudge back up to his building. The streets are slushy and dotted with people, shuffling along with hoods up and heads down. He shakes the snow off your jacket as he takes it off you and hangs it up in his closet. "Movie night!" he chirps. "Unless I eat your skin first!"

You giggle while he fake-nibbles on your clothes, pulling

your shirt up and your pants down and leaving a sizable bite on your butt cheek that elicits a yelp. "Get naked and into bed," he growls, and bites again and you yelp again and comply.

When it's over, he goes to the bathroom and you're left waiting, until you realize that you should put your clothes back on and join him because he's already sitting in the living room on his computer.

"Hey," you say. "What was that flat X wood thing you were working on?"

"That," he says, pulling you onto his lap so you're facing away from him and wrapping his arms around you, "will be for tying girls up, on their backs, to be blindfolded and wheeled around and used. And maybe if you're very good you'll get to use it."

"I better," you say. You've never done anything like that before, but there's no reason you can't. You can close your eyes and hold still and know that nothing all that bad is going to happen to you. BDSM sex can be a lot like a roller coaster at an amusement park—strap in, do nothing, you're not going to get hurt.

"I'm thinking I'll paint it purple," he says. "With black dots. Or stripes."

And the fantasy is completely ruined. For whatever reason, having the X painted purple makes it all seem so cheap, and high school weirdo outcast who shops at Hot Topic. If it was just wood, or even black, it could be sex-party-in-the-Hamptons. But purple. When your homemade sex toy is painted purple, the connotation is bad wizard role-play.

"Okay," you say.

"Hey, have you ever seen *Freaked*? It's with the guy from *Bill and Ted* who's not Keanu Reeves."

"I have not."

"Okay, we are watching that right now. You are going to love it."

And because you love the idea of being with someone who knows what you'll love, you nestle into him on the couch and pretend to like even the gross bits of the B-horror comedy. You fall asleep in his bed while he's on the couch on his laptop, promising that he'll be in soon.

The next morning, the snow day is as bad as everyone thought it would be. For once, forecasters and fear mongering haven't left the city overprepared and unsatisfied under a quick flurry of snow that barely sticks. The floor-to-ceiling windows in the Lawyer's apartment are pure white and fizzling with the frantic energy of angry snow.

The Lawyer is asleep on the couch, with half a blanket over his legs. "Okay," you say, plopping down next to him and kissing him awake. "There is no way you can go meet your friend. Look outside the window." You had thought carefully of how to phrase it: playful, non-accusing, totally Cool Girl. You're pretty sure you nailed it.

He groans and rolls over, checks his phone, and then looks outside.

"It's not that bad. Besides, I still have an hour before I have to leave."

The rings on the table from water glasses are visible in the diffuse morning light. You can see the dust on his bookshelves. "I guarantee she's going to cancel. I mean, look at this," you say. It was white-out conditions through his windows. The only hint that the ground was still below you at all was a streetlight on the corner, barely visible and bravely glowing red through the snow for the benefit of a completely empty street.

The Lawyer checks his phone again. "Nope, still on. And the subways are running. See the news alerts?"

He flashes the screen at you. It says SEVERE DELAYS DUE TO FLOODING ON ALL LINES.

You only moved into your new apartment two days ago. You still don't know which subway line you take to get there from here and so while you get dressed you frantically plug the address into Google Maps. Luckily, a station for the 2/3 train is at the top of his block, less than five minutes away. It'll bring you to 96th and Broadway, two blocks from your new home.

"You haven't seen my new apartment yet," you say.

"Well, you're going to be there for a while, aren't you?" he replies, buttoning his shirt.

"It's off the 2/3 line," you offer, hoping your disappointment comes across, that he's actually leaving, that you're actually leaving, without sounding needy. A girl is never supposed to be needy. Not even during blizzards.

"Great, I'll walk you," he says. And the two of you ride in silence down his elevator and brace yourselves the moment his building's doors groan open and eject you into the wind and slush and blinding snow that tears at your exposed skin and begins creeping its dampness into every crevice.

You aren't sure exactly which direction the subway stop on the map is located, but you're almost positive the Lawyer begins setting out in the wrong direction. He knows the neighborhood, you think. He knows where the closest subway stop is. And so even as the two of you trudge through the frozen tundra, along abandoned streets and sidewalks only shared by the foolish, for ten, then fifteen minutes you don't say anything. Your hands tingle with numbness at the fingertips, and you'd reach for the Lawyer's hand if it didn't mean an excruciating moment of your hand not being in your pocket. All you can do is follow him, eyes nearly shut, step after step, knowing that you're in good hands and if you just follow along you're not going to get hurt and, like a roller coaster, everything is going to work out.

Finally, from the tiny gap of street you can see beneath the hood pulled over your face and the ground, you see the forest green of a subway sign with the promise that the train below will take you to Manhattan. When he kisses you on the head to say goodbye, it all seems worth it. This kiss has the tenderness of a romantic hero. Lovers kiss their women on the forehead. You are his, and he has delivered you safely to the subway station, even if it is one, you realize now, full stop farther along on the train's route than the station that would have required just half a block of backtracking.

There are four of you on the subway (mercifully running without delays), all dripping onto the floor and shivering in wet, heavy coats. You all stare straight ahead in silence. None of you were supposed to leave the house today. This is one of the blizzards that grinds New York City to a standstill, freezes its taxicabs and halal carts in place while its residents stay in their apartments performing a hundred thousand mini-pantomimes in which they are the type of people who play board games and make hot chocolate on the stove.

When you get back to your new apartment, your roommate is sitting on the floor, in a corner, propped up with pillows and reading a book. Neither of you have furniture yet—the only light in the room is the sun coming through the two narrow windows on the southern side of the apartment that looks out onto an alley and a brick wall. You shake your boots off and smile and pull a blanket out of one of your boxes and flatten it on the floor, and then add your pillows to the pile. You smile and pretend as though this was how you wanted to spend the snow day after all. In a way, it was. The two of you sit together on the blanket on the floor, curled under an unwashed comforter, and watch Netflix on your laptop while you grab alternating handfuls of popcorn and Australian licorice. And when the light from the windows becomes dimmer, you make hot chocolate on the stove, using what you have (almond milk, cocoa powder, Splenda) and clink your glasses together, toasting to the snow day.

Objectively, he fucked you over on this one. If a friend described this scenario you would instantly transform into Samantha from *Sex and the City*. "Honey, dump the dummy," you'd say in your drawling Kim Cattrall voice. "Even if his jury was…hung."

Do you break it off with the Lawyer?

A. Yes. He doesn't get your sense of humor, making you feel dumb every time you try to make a joke, and then even dumber for being willing to dumb yourself down for him. Plus, he couldn't even spend a blizzard with you without going on another date. He's not The One, whatever that is.

Turn to page 206.

B. No. You've already told your friends that you were seeing someone, and he's the first person you've met in New York City who seems to genuinely like and understand you. Or at least, that's willing to continually sleep with you. You can make it work; you just need to communicate better.

Turn to page 215.

TINDER FILLS A HUMAN NEED, a need as palpable as thirst or hunger or taking an Instagram picture of your brunch so you can let the outside world know you were able to drag your ass out of bed at noon on a Sunday and spend $16 on eggs. Tinder fills our need for attention, to be *seen* by someone, to be wanted, and to not quite know what will happen next. It's a slot machine pass that you always win: Put in a bit of time and a few swipes, crank the lever, and out comes a parade of choices of people who might call you pretty and say they want to buy you a drink. The need strikes you at different times, usually after you've been drinking with a friend, or spending too much time on social media, when you're lonely and scrolling through Twitter and realizing every guy you follow is married or gay or both and that, upon checking your phone, no one has reached out with even the offer of a booty call. No one wants you. But you can change that.

It's midnight on a Thursday and you open Tinder.

You swipe right on Kyle because he went to an Ivy League school and although you can't exactly see his full face in the three pictures he offered, it seems like he had a good head of hair and nice, blue eyes. None of his pictures show him with a gun. He seems *fine*, and he's also on the Upper West Side, which means you'd be spared the inevitable midnight subway ride home alone from a mediocre date when you realize you want to escape as soon as possible.

Fuck it, what do you have to lose? "Hey," you type, and the message from him comes back immediately.

"How's it going?"

Generic, but harmless. It seems you have swiped right on the taupe wallpaper of people.

"Oh, you know," you type back. You're emboldened by the version of him you're building in your mind: bookish, lonely, way too excited that a girl messaged him first. You attempt to reshape yourself into the flirtatious, fearless ingénue you're pretty sure he wants, but you still only manage a, "Bored, spending the night in."

"So let's go out."

Your eyebrows rise. It's midnight. You didn't expect him to be quite so gutsy this early on. Tinder etiquette means you exchange a few awkward preliminaries on the app, flirt atrociously, then exchange numbers. If the texting doesn't fizzle out in a few days, *then* the two of you play chicken until one of you suggests a date. On the off chance neither of you cancels before (a sure sign the date will never be rescheduled), the two of you will meet in public.

"Now?" you respond. "It's midnight." Your hair isn't washed. You already took off your bra.

Do you go on the date?

A. Yes. This is New York, baby! Time to be young and impulsive and do things that objectively sound awful—like say, putting on your bra.

Continue reading.

B. No. You can always meet up with him another time when you're a little bit more desperate.

Turn to page 226.

"Why not?" he types back immediately. "I'll come to you."

There are a thousand reasons why not, but you've been in your bedroom, in a nest of unwashed sheets for days. You are starved for human attention, to feel attractive, to flirt with someone who isn't the Lawyer. You sent him two texts yesterday, in a moment of weakness, one asking him if he wanted to hang out and then, an hour later when the first yielded no response, sending along a toothless, "hope you have a great weekend!" He never replied, and you, cheeks burning, deleted the conversation from your phone as if by not having to look at it you could pretend it never happened. He is probably out with one of his female friends that he may or may not be sleeping with. And you are alone, with no one to text.

Romantic comedy heroines are always up for anything. Why can't you be too? You are young and you live in New York City and that means you should be doing more exciting things. You are constantly measuring yourself against the *idea* of what a young person in New York City should be doing, and you have had nowhere close to the requisite number of mischievous adventures. You pull a pair of jeans on that were turned inside out on your floor and wrestle your hair into a relatively acceptable ponytail. "There's a diner around the block from me," you write, and send him the name of the diner and the address.

"I'll be there in fifteen minutes," he writes back. "What's your number, in case I need to reach you?"

It's a normal request, but it catches you off guard. You wonder if he's been abandoned before by girls he's matched with on Tinder, if he's built this routine—meeting immediately, getting her phone number—as the only effective strategy to actually meeting women. Something about it feels ominous, a little overbearing for the boy you had assumed was passive, nerdy, desperate to please. But it's too late now. You're meeting him in fifteen minutes and your pants are on. What do you have to lose? You give him your number and leave your house exactly fifteen minutes later so you'll arrive at the diner a minute or two after him and make him wait.

As soon as you see him, you know you've made a mistake. He's wearing a newsboy flat cap, and his button-down shirt is rumpled and stained at the hem. He's tall, but gangly in a way that makes his entire posture resemble the letter C. When he smiles, a row of tiny, yellow teeth stare out at you. He is not your type.

Luckily, you're around the corner from your house. You are here to get to know someone, and then you never have to see him again. Maybe it won't be that bad.

Even though you'd only just confirmed the date, he seems surprised when you walk in. He rises and you, still in romantic comedy heroine persona, reach in to give him a hug, a thank-you for coming all the way to your neighborhood. You have never been in this diner before but you find, to your surprise, it's not entirely off-putting, even after midnight. There's comfort in its archetypal diner-ness. There are a few other patrons at tables, sitting in silent Edward Hopper tableaus. The menus are thick, vinyl, and slightly sticky.

There's a rotating display of mostly-intact pies glowing in the fluorescent light of the counter.

The two of you sit in a booth and mercifully he removes the hat. You smile politely and ask about his family. He orders pork chops with mashed potatoes and a side of steamed broccoli. You get a black coffee.

When the check comes, and he pays for your coffee with only the smallest gesture of benevolence, you give him a flirty smile and demurely say thank you. Sure, you could have paid for your own coffee, but you sat for twenty-five minutes pretending to be interested in his undergraduate thesis on Thoreau and his ex-girlfriend. You considered it a $2.50 tax for your presence. That was the point of ordering coffee in the first place: You are Cool New York girl, drinking her coffee on a date, not allowing herself to get invested but taking what's given to her.

"All right, I think it's time for me to head back home," you say, pulling your coat over your shoulders. He wiggles his cap back on.

"Do you want to take a walk for a bit?" he asks. "Even just around the block."

He isn't awful; you could at least give him that. And the way he asked for a walk seemed almost sweet, if it didn't verge on pathetic. Anyway, you just drank coffee, and you aren't sleepy. Sure. You could go on a walk with him. Maybe he'd flirt and you could go to bed with a full tank of attention. But, you don't want to.

"It's late," you say in a tone meant to shut him down. It isn't an eyebrow-waggling, "It's late," delivered from underneath your eyelashes with an implicit dot dot dot at the end, but more of an exhausted-housewife-who-is-planning-on-leaving-her-husband-and-turning-down-his-half-hearted-attempt-to-initiate-sex-after-fifteen-years-of-marriage "It's late."

"Just around the block," he says, and you are tired, but you have nothing else to do except surf the Internet mindlessly in bed, and you've done that every night more or less for the last three years.

"Okay."

And the two of you walk on the darkened sidewalk beneath the construction scaffolding that's been there since you've moved to this neighborhood, and although he pulls the usual seduction moves—alluding to his own sexual prowess in a way you just know he thinks is casual, brushing his hand slightly against your leg—you are so uninterested they come across as almost comical. You're like a kindergarten teacher smiling at a five-year-old student who tells you he has a crush on you.

Eventually, you reach the logical point where he seems to expect a kiss and you offer a stern but polite, "Maybe another night. No, I'm sorry, maybe another night," before walking with long Girl Power strides back to your apartment, opening the door, and mentally confirming that you'll never see him again.

One of your friends is a Tinder maniac, swiping and matching endlessly and arriving at every brunch the two of you have with a new story and a new boy's first name. This week, it's Aaron, a six-foot-tall Australian finance bro. Last time, it was a count (an actual count) from England who she dumped when she slowly realized he was a quiet Trump supporter.

For you, Tinder is just the Uber of mediocre dates, on demand, just a swipe and a click away. When you first arrived in New York, you made plans with a boy who had promised unparalleled proclivity as a BDSM dom, until you brought him back to your room, got on all fours, and realized he immediately came on your leg without even entering you. And then there was the boy you met in SoHo, a cute redhead with an athletic build who you knew within fifteen minutes of meeting that you weren't sexually attracted to. When he suggested the two of you head back to his place (a subway transfer and a bus ride away) and you declined, citing a headache, he stormed out of the bar without even paying his bill.

The truth about Tinder is that it behaves like any vice: never as enjoyable as your craving made it seem. You were bored and empty and hungry for attention, and then you swipe until men seem interchangeable and even more boring than the alternative: watching Netflix alone. The foreplay before a date—the flirting, the texting, the speculation— becomes rote and stale, and it always deflates right when you see the guy in person, sitting at the bar in terrible jeans, shorter than he looked in his pictures, probably wearing a douchey necklace or something.

Back when you were bingeing and gaining weight in college, you decided that your vice would be smoking instead. The idea was to exchange one vice for another, and if you were successful, at least you would be skinny. Cancer you could deal with later—you were twenty, and thus invincible to all of that—but the shame of always feeling like the ugly girl was killing you *now*.

They said cigarettes were supposed to kill your appetite and dull your taste buds, but turns out those weren't the reasons you were bingeing in the first place. If you weren't hungry, you just chose more tempting foods—fattier, saltier, new, different—and ate until you needed to throw up. Then you'd try, and regardless of how successful the attempt was, you'd move on to round two of your bingeing. Hunger didn't factor in, and, surprise surprise, neither did taste. Ho Hos and Doritos are chemically designed to bypass straight to the pleasure center of your brain: They'd still taste good if your tongue was made of cardboard.

Maybe if you could have smoked in bed, while you were mindlessly surfing the Internet. They say to break a habit you need to replace it, and that was where you binged, like a rat in its nest, curled up with a fully charged screen and a full bag of treats in the crook between your comforter and the wall. But the dorm rooms had smoke detectors and you hated the thought of anything you owned smelling like cigarettes, and so you smoked twice on the stoop outside your building and felt too fat and too self-conscious to pull off the "nonchalant smoker" thing.

You knew if you were thin, smoking would have been cool: Your jeans would hang from your ass and your T-shirt would show off your collarbone and the messy heap of hair you wrangled into a bun would somehow look elegant and serve to show off your perfect profile. And while you were not necessarily ugly—you looked pretty from some angles, in some lights, but definitely swollen—you were sure you came across as vaguely pathetic, just inexpertly sucking on a cigarette until you stomped it out with an inch left to smoke.

The habit didn't catch on. You got through half the pack before you gave it to a smoker who lived in your dorm, a filmmaking student with legs up to his ears and a penchant for wearing suspenders and women's hats. "Really?" he said, his hands already extended to take the gift. "You really want to give them to me?" You did. You never bought a pack of cigarettes again, but you would spend years going on terrible Tinder dates. It was the only vice that ever matched the quick spike of dopamine that came with bingeing foods packaged in plastic. Besides, if you got home from your date early, you could have your cake too.

Turn to page 226.

NEW YORK CITY, YOU FIND, is a series of odd jobs and emails about how the two of you *finally need* to meet for coffee (you never will) and procrastination and killing cockroaches, actual cockroaches the size of both of your thumbs put together in your tiny Manhattan apartment. You had assumed this was just New York City folklore that happened to everyone except you, like getting an STD or having to take the G train. It wasn't.

For this odd job, you are on the third floor of an unmarked office building in Long Island City, with a stand-up comedian you know through a friend of a friend and the producer who brought you both here, with her laptop open, asking you to brainstorm penis jokes. Well, dildo jokes, specifically. The next episode of MTV's Snapchat show is about sex toys, and because you are fifteen months out of college and spend far too much time on Twitter, the general population assumes you understand Snapchat. The truth (which you did tell the producer, who shrugged) is that you have no idea how Snapchat operates beyond its basic functions and have no understanding of its appeal. You downloaded it and deleted it and re-downloaded it a handful of times, but it seems like a complicated step to add to your social media rotation. How are you supposed to remember your friends' usernames? Are you supposed to already know your friends' usernames? If you see something funny, how do you know whether you're supposed to Snapchat it, or Tweet it, or Instagram it, or just text the image to the one friend that you actually want to see it? "You just *know*," your little sister scoffs. She is twenty and a college sophomore and sends so many Snapchats a day it seems mathematically impossible that she isn't constantly looking at life through her phone.

You don't want to become a stereotype of a crotchety octogenarian, proselytizing about the Good Old Days when people just *talked* to each other goddammit, and when you didn't need to remember all of these goddamn buttons to just send a simple message. You don't want to become one of those people who wear their technological ignorance with a prideful superiority either: "I just don't understand all of those FaceTweets!" and all of that. You want to be Cool and In The Know and Trendy and, if possible, Internet Famous. You just don't have the mental energy to catch up on something you're already so far behind on when instead you can curl into a metaphorical ball and only let it graze you on the surface level.

"Dildo jokes? Anyone?" the producer asks. The comedian brings up how there's a town called Dildo, maybe somewhere in Montana.

"That's *perfect*," the producer says. "We can do like, a little animation with a Welcome to Dildo town sign."

"All of the town buildings can be dildos," the comedian says.

"Amazing," the producer says, typing.

You have your laptop open to a website listing fun facts about dildos. You are contemplating bringing up a diamond-encrusted dildo worth $13 million (that can't be... comfortable) when you get the ding of a Facebook notification. It's from the Lawyer.

"Yeah, I don't think I can come to the thing tonight," the message reads.

You type back immediately. "????? what's wrong"

"The thing" is a PR event at a clothing store whose wares you probably don't fit into, but those things have free drinks and free appetizers and you get to leave with a free hat or towel or flask that you'll throw away in three months. It's also a chance for you to arrive at an event with a tall boy on your arm, a boy with muscles visible through his shirt and a nice smile. And you—the girl he thinks is smart, the girl he prizes because she's successful and connected—will get to show off how comfortable you are flitting among the well-dressed *Gossip Girl* types and the PR flacks. Will he feel insecure, you wonder, about his lack of sophistication, his middling literary ideas, his friends who work at renaissance faires and not Ralph Lauren? Will he be impressed and filled with a sense of longing urgency, and love you more? Relationships are always about domination. At this, you have the upper hand.

"I just don't think I can make it."

"What do you mean," you type, trying to make it look like you are still Googling dildo facts. "I told you about this like, a week ago."

"Okay," his message pops up. And then a second message. "It just seems a little...relationship-y."

You become a hissing medusa in your mind, all of the tiny moments of proof that you have built a relationship flaring around your head like shrieking snakes poised to attack. *You are in a relationship!* the snakes hiss in unison. *You have been dating for months! You spend more nights at his apartment than your own! He cooked you dinner, he talked about taking you on a trip!*—but you are Cool Girl. You don't type any of that. You take a deep breath, and type: "If the party thing bothers you, it's not important at all. Let's do something else tonight." The snakes settle, disappointed, as you hit SEND.

Bubbles appear on the screen, indicating that he's typing, and then the bubbles stop. Then they appear again and you watch with the rapt attention of a woman possessed. The producer and the comedian have moved on to discussing butt plugs. The Lawyer's message finally comes through: "I don't think that's really the issue."

"What is the issue?"

"Danaaaaaaa." It was written but you can hear him saying it, the exasperation and the condescension in his voice. "Okay. Fine. You wrote about being jealous about me sleeping with someone else. You were the one who asked if I wanted a threesome the other night!"

You pause. How do you explain every version of yourself to someone who's barely met you? You've written about your jealousy—tweets, a short piece for a freelance publication online, all with his identity obscured—and tried to reconcile dating a man who's polyamorous with your own insecurity, with the visions you get of him fucking and falling in love with a girl skinnier than you, with prettier eyes and good abs and hamstrings that don't prevent her from touching her toes. You were exorcising your sins to the online public, turning your faults into quirky, relatable content. Being jealous feels less awful when it gets a hundred favorites, a hundred beeps of recognition, of "This is normal. I feel the same way." And you get to feel above it all for writing about it, because nothing can be really that painful if it's put in a jokey tweet.

The threesome offer came when you were Cool Girl,

when you were in bed beside him, one of the rare instances when you fell asleep together. You put on your best R-rated Zooey Deschanel impression: "Tell me all of your secrets. Tell me your fetishes. Threesome? Want to have a threesome? We can have a threesome." The words weren't an offer so much as an offering. *Put me on your team*, they pleaded. *I will do anything as long as we are doing it alongside one another.* He had his knives and his Velcro restraints under his bed and you had your words, verbal parries and retreats, weak as paper airplanes hitting a brick wall.

You weigh your options and decide on surrender: "I do get jealous. It's something I have to deal with. I'm sorry." White flag, belly up, being a sub is about giving up control, and maybe it's the same with being in a relationship with a dom.

His response comes so quick you know that he'd already typed it out: "This isn't working. It was always supposed to be a sex thing."

You are still sitting in the random conference room, with two strangers, pretending to be a cool, competent, funny millennial, and you start to cry. Real, heavy tears, building and dropping, heavy as water balloons. "Ugh, allergies," you say to the room. The producer and the comedian don't look too closely at you.

How do you write back?

A. A full retreat. Go back to the last save point in the game, keep spending time with him, make him like you more: *You're right. You're right. I've been reading into things but I get it. Just sex. Let's talk about this in person, but you're right.*

Turn to page 221.

B. Press your tongue against the rotting tooth, just to make sure it hurts: *So, what? Are you just breaking up with me on Facebook message?*

Turn to page 222.

YOU'RE TRYING NOT TO CRY, really, really trying. But the game isn't over. "You're right," you type. "You're right. I've been reading into things but I get it. Just sex. Let's talk about this in person, but you're right."

His gray text bubbles appear, and you hold your breath, and then his message comes through: "I don't think that's a good idea."

Now the rage comes through. "What? Meeting in person or still having sex?"

"Both of those. Maybe in a week when you cool down we can get coffee or something."

Turn to page 223.

"SO, WHAT? ARE YOU JUST BREAKING UP WITH ME ON FACEBOOK MESSAGE?"

Do it, you chant silently. Just fucking do it. You walk straight into the knife and lean to the side so he doesn't have to go through the effort of twisting it. Make it hurt.

"I think you feel like this relationship is something it isn't," the response comes. Tiny letters attached to someone whose face you can't see.

Turn to page 223.

YOU COULD ARGUE, bring up the nights you cuddled and watched movies, the Home Depot runs, the smiles and the "I'm really starting to like you's." But said knife has already punctured your small intestine and your tears are stinging and the anger has nowhere to go but through your fingers and straight back into you.

"SO you're breaking up with me," you write. "So that's it."

"Well, jeez, if you want to put it like that. I still like you. I want to be friends. But I just don't think we should be having sex anymore."

And so your non-relationship that was only about sex can't even be about that anymore. You are unloved and unwanted and soon to be ignored.

"Dana?" the producer asks. "Did you want to take the cock rings section?"

"Yeah," you murmur, "I just need to run to the bathroom quickly." You bring your phone and keep your head down so no one in the hallway will see your flushed cheeks and wet, fluorescent-pink eyes.

"Oh btw," another message from him comes through. "If you want to, let me know if your writing publishing people are looking for other pitches. I feel like I could write a piece about the jealousy thing, but from my side."

You can't quite laugh and cry at the same time, and if the wound didn't still hurt, you would have smiled. That message is the best parting gift anyone has ever given you. The guy dumped you on Facebook chat, and then had the gall to ask you for your connections. He is so instantly and unambiguously the villain in the story. Those two details are so easy to pull out, at brunch, in tweets, in one-sided storytelling with a clear and straightforward thesis: "Once I dated a bad man, a dumb bad man." There is no fault to be parsed out, no introspection necessary, when he made such a fatal error in victory. (Months later, he will make another glorious, unforced error: He will ask you, via wonderfully screenshot-able text message, if you might be willing to resend the naked pictures you had sent throughout your relationship, as currency, bribes for attention. His phone broke, you see, and its trove of content with it. It doesn't matter that the two of you had, at that point, made up, or he might have been mostly joking, probably flirting just a little, teasing to try his luck. It still gives you the brilliantly sympathetic role in a funny story: the victim of a clueless douchebag of an ex-boyfriend.)

Relationships are all about domination. You have the last word in a way. Nothing was your fault, and even though now you are crying and unlovable and alone, you don't need to ask yourself what you did wrong. Your only mistake, you'll say, three days later over mimosas with your most sympathetic friend—in a ritual of performative basicness, of pretend *Sex and the City*—was not breaking up with him first.

But you aren't ready to tease out the story of your relationship just then, when you are in the bathroom in the office building in Long Island City. You come out lightheaded, with red eyes, and say again, "Ugh, the worst allergies. I am so, so sorry," praying they'll either be oblivious enough to believe you or tactful enough not to ask while you get back to your computer and put out there that it might qualify as a fun fact that the vibrator was invented in the Victorian Era.

Turn to page 206.

"BEING SOCIAL REQUIRES EFFORT," your mom would always tell you. "Sometimes you need to just take a shower, blow-dry your hair, put on a pair of jeans, and go out even when you don't feel like it."

Tonight, you don't feel like it. The party—a housewarming—is in the lower bowels of Brooklyn, somewhere optimistically still labeled "Bushwick" that requires a subway transfer and a twenty-two-minute walk. But you're young, you tell yourself. You have two working legs. You're a twenty-three-year-old in New York City, and that means you're supposed to have a social life. And so you force yourself to go to a party that starts at 10:00 p.m., even though you sincerely believe that 10:00 p.m. is when every party should end.

You hadn't worried about not bringing a gift until you were half a block away. Do recent college grads give each other housewarming gifts? It feels like we're all moving between walk-ups and sublets so often, there would just be an unceasing wheel of regifting novelty kitchen knickknacks. But you could have brought a bottle of wine or something. Too late now—you're at the threshold and it's time for your fake high-pitched voice to come out, your "Oh my God, you look so good!" and "This place is amazing!" Hugs are exchanged, introductions are made, and then you're sitting on a couch trying to keep yourself from eating too much Brie even though there's Brie right there in front of you and you already ate some so tonight is a lost cause; there's no use trying to be healthy anymore until tomorrow morning.

Do the rest of the girls notice how much Brie you've been eating? Is the party secretly judging you, the girl who came in without even contributing a bottle of wine? You watch other people for how much *they've* eaten and try to not be the person who's eaten the most even though you're almost positive you are.

The rest of these girls have known each other longer than you have. They name-drop editors and old friends and you smile along. "I'm so glad we got this space," your hostess coos. "Rob wanted us to find somewhere we would get a decent enough kitchen so we could cook."

"It's amaaaaazing," the rest of you purr back. She and her boyfriend had been dating for a year and decided to move in together. You dated the Lawyer for four months and he didn't even want to meet your friends.

There is no more Brie. You might have eaten it all. You can't remember. Three new girls come through the door, and all three of them brought their own bottle of wine to offer. Your cheeks flush and suddenly you feel very claustrophobic, stuck between people trying to talk to you. You cannot learn any more names or make any more small talk. You down the plastic glass of champagne you had been given and pour yourself another. You drink that one, too, and then you look up the train route to get home. You just want to be in your bed. You would give your left arm and your life savings for the power of teleportation at that moment, for you just to snap your fingers and be back behind your own door where you could take off your pants, forget about Brie and girls with boyfriends that love them, and just watch YouTube videos until you fall asleep. You feel very, very deep into Brooklyn.

There are train delays. Google Maps says to get home you'd need to take a subway and two buses, and the trip would take an hour and twenty-five minutes. You could cry. You open Uber and punch in your address. *Surge pricing!* a pop-up advises. To make it home, it would take fifty minutes and cost $70. You have $96 in your checking account. You are stranded among smiling, drunk acquaintances very far from home. You've plunged yourself into your own personal nightmare.

Then you have a quick spark of inspiration. That mediocre guy you matched with on Tinder—Kevin or whatever—he went to Columbia. He lives on the Upper West Side. You could just meet him. You could have sex tonight. That would be fine. Or you could just say you're too tired and sleep at his place. But you can get him to pay for your Uber. And then at least you won't be here anymore.

"Heyyy," you text him. "Still up?"

"Yup," comes the reply. "What are you up to?"

"At a boring party in Brooklyn. You?"

"Home."

Perfect.

He beats you to the punchline: "Want to come over?"

"Yessssss," you reply. The extra s's are to make you seem drunker and sluttier than you are. "But the trains are all delayed:("

"Uber?" he replies. He has a fish on the line and he's not going to let you go.

"Wanna get me an Uber to your place?" you type. "Pay for my Uber and I'm yours."

You're playacting the seductress, the sensual escort who comes to a nervous boy's house with an air of sophistication and sexual prowess. This boy is sweet, playing exactly into your hands. You almost pity him—sleeping with him will be an act of benevolence.

"What's the address of the party?" he types back.

The two of you text the entire car ride to his apartment as you bump along in the black sedan toward Manhattan. "What color panties are you wearing?" he texts. The word *panties* grosses you out. You wish he wasn't the type of person who said that sort of thing. But you're already in a car headed toward his place; it's too late for that. "Purple lace," you type. "Need someone to rip them off me."

His apartment is thirty blocks north of yours, past Morningside Heights and up into an area that qualifies as Harlem, all concrete and flimsy gray buildings and neon lights and closed storefronts. The driver isn't exactly sure which building on the block is the destination. "It's okay," you say. "I'll just get out here."

When you step outside, under the shadow of an overpass and across the street from an out-of-business Papa John's, you realize how dumb it is to be in this neighborhood, alone, at one in the morning. You aren't sure which apartment is Kevin's either, and so you walk a bit away from the main road and try to make out the addresses in the darkness.

Finally, after a few minutes of waiting in the dark, you call him, and a few minutes later, you see a figure approaching from a building a few doors down.

"You're actually here," he says with surprise in his voice. He gestures to his phone. "I saw the Uber had arrived but I didn't see you."

"Well, I'm here," you say.

"Excellent. Let me show you the way up."

His apartment is a studio, with a cheap polyester com-

forter over an unmade bed—a bed on plastic risers, like
in a college dorm. It's separated from his living room by a
Japanese-style divider, and on the other side, a television set
sits crooked on an end table. You take a seat on the couch,
and Kevin sits close to you, offering a drink and gently
touching the skin on your thigh with the back of his fingers.
You decline. You're only a few hours out from the first glass
of champagne but you're beginning to feel the symptoms of
an eventual hangover—you're drunk still but a headache
is blooming. Your limbs all feel heavy. You wish you were
home, but you're here now, and you might as well make the
best of it.

"Do you have some water?" you ask. "And an Advil or
something?"

He sighs and gets up and returns with two midnight-blue gel
pills in his palm. They're Advil PM, but it doesn't matter. It's
night anyway, and if you fall asleep, you won't have to have sex
with him. You take both pills and swallow them dry.

"I am soooo tired," you say.

"I don't mind," he replies. He doesn't look away from your
face. "Hey, did you ever role-play?"

"What sort of stuff do you have in mind?"

"Oh, you know," he says. "Typical daddy/little girl stuff.
But I do have this one fantasy." He moves his hand farther
up your thigh and you don't move it. "Has anyone ever told
you that you look like Lena Dunham?"

People, unfortunately, have told you that you look like
Lena Dunham. You don't particularly take it as a
compliment—aside from being slightly chubby with a Jewish nose, you don't look very much alike at all. People saying
you look like Lena Dunham is a socially acceptable way for

people to say, "Hey, if you were famous, people would say it's brave for you to wear a bathing suit in public!"

"Yeah?" you offer. You are not entirely a fan of wherever this is going.

"Well," he says, "I have this fantasy that you're Lena Dunham and I'm your daddy who's so proud of my successful, artistic, creative little girl."

You don't say, "That sounds a little weird." You do say, "I'm really tired. I think I'm going to lie down."

You don't know how long you were asleep before you feel him on top of you, peeling off his T-shirt and pants until he's just wearing boxers, the tip of his penis peeking through their slit. "Take off your panties," he whispers. You do. You'll have sex with him, you think, and you'll get it over with.

He begins rubbing his erection between your legs. "Do you have a condom?" you whisper through the haze of alcohol and sleepiness.

"Shhhhh, don't worry about it," he says.

"No, no," you say. "You have to put on a condom."

"Just go back to sleep," he says, and you try to acquiesce because you don't want to be here right now, but his pumping is awkward and painful and his hands are clammy and overeager. You try to push him off but he holds your wrists down and grins with relish. "That's it, my little girl. My talented little Lena."

What do you do?

A. You try to leave.

Continue reading.

You've forgotten the word for *stop* and you're not entirely sure he'd pay attention anyway. And so you say the one thing that comes to mind: "I have to pee. Get off me, I have to pee."

He reluctantly complies, and you waddle your way to his filthy bathroom, a room so small that if you closed the door while sitting on the toilet it would graze your knees. But Kevin follows you to the bathroom and he doesn't close the door.

"I have to pee," you whisper. You realize how drunk you still are—you think it's drunkenness that's causing the room to spin and your head to bob.

"I know," he murmurs. "I know, little girl. But I have to watch."

"No," you say. "I'm okay." The truth is you don't have to pee; you just wanted to get away from him, and now he's right there, blocking your way out and you're sitting on the toilet with nothing to do but look up at him.

"I have to watch. I have to know if you're okay."

You're not sure if the entire thing is part of the fetish, that he likes watching girls pee, or if he knows you're drunk and drowsy on sleeping medication and he's worried you'll crack your head open on the tiling or something.

Eventually, a tiny stream trickles out, and you take longer than normal to wash your hands before you head back to his bed. "I'm really tired," you say, and lie on your back.

"I know, baby," he says, and he crawls on top of you.

He's lying next to you when you wake up again, the sun barely managing to brighten the room through dusty windows on the opposite wall. You go to the bathroom, pee, and let the remnants of the night before drip from your body into the water below with a sickening plop. You pull on your shoes and take your phone and purse while he rouses himself. "Do you want me to make you a cup of coffee?" he asks. You look at your phone. It's seven in the morning.

"No, thank you," you reply, and dragging your coat behind you, you try to leave his apartment. He has to come over to help you with the latch.

"Maybe we can do this again sometime," he says.

"Maybe," you say, holding back tears. You're still dizzy as you make your way down three sets of stairs and then press out onto the shining concrete outside.

You speed-walk to Broadway, farther north than you've ever been on Broadway, and after five minutes of frantically pacing, you find a cab going the wrong way and you make it do a U-turn. It takes twenty minutes to get down to your house.

When you finally get home, you peel your clothes off and squat in the shower, scrubbing every inch of your skin with scalding hot water. You want to turn your skin inside out and clean the fleshy pink underside of your skin too. You want your entire body to be created out of new cells.

You don't tell anyone what happened, and when you eventually do, it's only the barest details. You're sure the more of the story you tell, the more your friends will believe what you secretly believe: that it was all your own stupid fault.

You text him a few days later, asking him to delete your number, telling him you hadn't consented to him not using a condom, to fucking you in the ass (had he fucked you in the ass?), to using your body when you were asleep.

"I am so, so sorry you feel that way," he replied. "Genuinely, I never meant to do anything wrong. I thought that was what you wanted. Hadn't you been talking about the

BDSM stuff? But if you feel that way, I can only genuinely say that was not my intent."

You read it once, and then delete all evidence of him from your phone. He makes the bile curdle in your throat.

More as a masochistic thought exercise than anything, you imagine the courtroom trial if you were ever to report anything that happened. You see his lawyer, looking at you with no kindness in his eyes, while your parents watch from the courtroom seats behind him.

Do you recognize this text message? the lawyer would ask. *Did you say "pay for my Uber and I'm yours?"*

What did you mean by that?

Did you tell him what panties you were wearing?

Did you voluntarily go up to his apartment?

Have you ever taken an Advil PM before?

So you know what they look like?

And you took it voluntarily when he offered.

Did you get into his bed?

Did you ever say you wanted to leave?

Did you call a cab to get home?

Was he keeping you hostage? You were only thirty blocks away from your house. A smart girl like you didn't call a cab to go home?

Did you file a report with the police the following morning?

No further questioning, Your Honor.

You are a slut who had bad sex with a skeevy guy and regretted it. All of the guilt, all of the shame, that feeling that you want to leave your skin that no showers in the world will ever make you clean, face it: All of that anger is for you, not him. The perfect cap on the worst version of yourself that you became.

A few years ago, you went on a trip to Rome with your dad. Between the sightseeing and pasta dinners, you were still freelancing, and you published a story about how you faked orgasms during sex. Your dad read it, and when you tried to play it off as a cool, normal thing for a young writer to do, demystifying female sex, making it less taboo, he began to cry.

You couldn't remember ever seeing your father cry before. "I can't help but think...," he managed to get out. The words were choking and difficult. "I can't help but think, that if I had been a better dad, if I had paid more attention..." He doesn't need to finish the sentence. If he had been a better dad, you wouldn't be as promiscuous as you are. You started to cry too. Your dad had been there for every single major event in your life. He took you to bookstores nearly every weekend. You went to the midnight release of *Harry Potter* books, the two of you wore matching Harry Potter glasses. He and your mom have been married for nearly thirty years. He has never not been there for you, and he's crying because he's ashamed of you. The two of you cried in that hotel in Rome for a few minutes, without talking.

You think about that now and you cry, alone in your shower. The water is off, but you crouch there, in the tub, soaking wet. What have you become? So hungry for affection or attention or excitement that you walk into the lion's den with your thong already at your ankles. You delete his number from your phone, but you can't delete his name or face from your mind. He was wearing a dumb fucking hat when he met you in the diner. He had a wheedling, annoying, high-pitched voice. He had thin hair. He was so greedy at the prospect of a girl in his bed that he would take her, struggling and then unconscious, unwilling to confront the tiny part of himself that knew she wasn't playing a game anymore, that she needed a glass of water and a blanket placed on top of her instead of a heaving, flabby white belly.

You went to see a man like that. You got in his bed. You allowed him to come inside you, and you will never, ever be able to scrub it out.

HEY, DO YOU WANT TO
DATE DANA SCHWARTZ?

Things are going fine.

Really.

You have a job, and friends you can talk to, and a nice apartment, and a roommate who is far neater than you but doesn't get mad when you leave water glasses all over the kitchen.

You go to your job, usually a little late, and then you take the subway home, order in dinner, and eat while watching Netflix, and then you browse the Internet in bed until you fall asleep and do it all again.

And then, an email from an editor—a *major* editor at a real publishing house. They like one of your Twitter accounts, the one where you make fun of dystopian young adult novels that all have blended together in a post–*Hunger Games* world. ("I have been Chosen, and I will not be Sorted into your Groups in this Society that Needlessly Capitalizes Nouns"!) The editor says she likes your voice. "Have you ever thought about writing a young adult novel?"

You write back immediately: You would love to try.

After two meetings in their chrome office building (you wear a new dress and heels for the first time since you've

moved to New York), you and the editor come up with an out-
line: a story about a high school girl who travels to Europe,
coincidentally to most of the same countries you happened
to visit when you graduated college. You write a sample
chapter and wait.

And wait.

And wait.

And then, one day, you get a phone call that begins with
the magic words "Are you sitting down?" and your agent
tells you that they loved the chapter and they want to buy the
book. "Congratulations," he says, and you can tell that he's
grinning through the phone. "You got a book deal!"

You mention it to relative strangers in the office of the *Late
Show* as you restock sodas, as casually as you possibly can
shoehorn it in. *Have a good weekend? Read any good books
lately? Funny you should mention books...*

On your days off, you set up with a large cup of black
coffee and a seat near a power outlet at the wood-paneled
cash-only hipster coffee shop only two blocks from your
house, and type furiously, letting each satisfying click of the
keyboard propel you on to the next sentence, the next paragraph, the next page.

Sometimes you wake up in the middle of the night just to
keep writing.

Sometimes you go days without being able to think of a
single word.

Eventually, you finish something you wouldn't be completely embarrassed to call a first draft and send it along,
and wait for the revisions to come back. The process repeats.
There is a lot of waiting, and even more waiting before your
book will finally come out, in the spring of next year.

You are okay.

But you are lonely. The same gnawing need for attention brings you back to Tinder but every profile makes you profoundly uncomfortable. Everyone is a sleaze bag only showing their good angles. You don't want to date strangers in New York City. You wish you could date people chosen from the pool of your Twitter followers, the people you technically spend the most time with anyway, the people who seem to accept the strange, self-indulgent idiosyncrasies of your personality.

And so, at 10:30 on a Thursday night, you make a Google form and jauntily title it "hey do you want to date dana schwartz?" The all lowercase is meant to seem relaxed and detached about it. You wouldn't want to seem desperate while making an online dating website only for you. You attempt the same nonchalance with the questions—nothing too serious or probing, nothing that could ruin the defensive facade you were building if no one responded that all of this was just a joke.

---

hey, do you want to date dana schwartz?

yes, i want to date writer/couch potato dana schwartz.

Name? _____

What do you do for a living? _____

How do you feel about dogs? _____

Are you willing to commute to the UWS to see me sometimes?

☐ Yes

☐ No

What is your most attractive quality?

_____

How do you feel about Tom Stoppard?

☐ Haven't read or seen much of him.

☐ Eh, I prefer Sarah Ruhl.

☐ Septimus, what is carnal embrace?

☐ I literally do not understand this question at all.

Other:

_____

Why do you want to date dana schwartz?

_____

What television show would you recommend we binge together?

_____

Do you think it's weird I'm attracted to Kylo Ren? Not Adam Driver. Kylo Ren the space Nazi.

☐ Yes

☐ No

☐ I'll accept you however you are.

☐ I'm actually Adam Driver, filling this out.

Other:

What's your Twitter handle?

_____

Actually give me an answer up there so i can ask you out bc i don't see ur email

☐ ok

Within two days, you have 200 replies. A dozen are from friends, people you know from school filling out the form with inside jokes. A majority are strangers from your Twitter, mostly older men or guys who live in distant red states, filling it out because filling out a form on the Internet is its own form of entertainment, flattering you but not actually proposing a relationship. A few people fill it out pretending (unfortunately) to be Adam Driver. But you look up everyone who responds, check their Twitter page for signs they might be a cute, halfway decent guy in New York City who happens to have a crush on you, probably because of all the tweets you do about Kenneth Branagh.

If the applicant passed the initial Twitter screening (no confederate flags, no anime avatars, at least one semidecent joke), the next step was to find them on Facebook. Mutual friends were a desperately sought-after bonus—and Charlie has four of them: three of your sister's friends from college and your sister. It looks like he has a job at a TV production company or something.

"Hey," you text said sister. "Do you know a guy Charlie _____ who went to Northwestern with you? He applied on my dating site."

Your older sister Caroline rolled her eyes but smiled when she saw the site. "I swear, you made this look like a joke, but I can tell you're seriously looking."

"Yeah," she writes back infuriatingly late. "He was cute."

"Nice?" you reply. "Normal?"

"I think so," she says.

Good enough. You follow him on Twitter and send him a DM. "So...do we go out on a date now? Not sure what the protocol for this is, but how about coffee?"

He replies immediately: "How about Sunday?"

There is another boy who makes it through your application process, a boy whose Twitter handle was a literary joke and who shares about half a dozen followers with you. From your stalking, he went to NYU, was in the sketch comedy group there, and interned at a literary journal. He works at the Barnes & Noble ten blocks from your apartment. He looks a little dorkier in his pictures than Charlie does— where Charlie is in tank tops and sunglasses at music festivals and hiking with his family, NYU Matt is making silly faces for the sketch group promotion pictures. There aren't enough pictures of him—after just a few clicks in his Facebook albums, you are back to high school, where he was just a stalk with bad skin and a haircut too close to his head.

Which boy do you want to go out with, or rather, which is the boy that you're going to marry and end up on the front page of the *New York Times* Vows section with, because how could you not when you have a story as cute as "We met on the silly dating app she created for herself?"

A. Charlie

Turn to page 243.

B. Matt

Turn to page 247.

HE'S SHORTER THAN YOU IMAGINED, but still incredibly cute when he smiles. You arrive at the coffee shop in SoHo early and decide to pose outside, one leg bent behind you, up against the wall so that when he arrives he finds you casual and scrolling through your phone.

"Hey!" he says, and hugs you. You get your coffees to go and bring them to a park nearby where you sit on a bench thigh to thigh.

"Yeah, I definitely think I knew your sister at school," he says. "That's so crazy."

"Such a small world."

It's the end of February, still a little too chilly to be sitting outside, but the sky is an unbroken spill of blue and the sun reflects off the creases of snow still left in gutters, which makes it almost look like spring.

You fish for the other few people you know in common. You talk about your jobs. And then, when you have nothing left to talk about, you both lean in at the exact same moment, the same resigned half-smile on your face, and begin to make out. It's a good enough kiss.

"This has been great," you say, before he does something dumb like invite you back to his place on a Sunday afternoon. "We should do this again sometime."

"How about drinks?" he says. "Saturday?"

Considering that this is a real Saturday night date from a real guy and not another night at home with

your laptop, you are elated. But there's a skinny literary heartthrob still waiting in the wings and the possibility of a better unknown is basically the basis of modern civilization. Is the grass actually greener? What do you do?

A. Go on another date with Charlie and see how it goes. A bird in the hand, and all of that. You know he's cute and non-crazy. When it comes to meeting strangers on the Internet, quit while you're ahead.

Continue reading.

B. Go out with Matt next week instead and cross all your fingers that he isn't a huge DFW fan.

Turn to page 247.

You know how in every romantic comedy, the leads who are certainly going to end up together begin the film by dating other people? Statistically it's Greg Kinnear or James Marsden. Sometimes it's their fiancée. This person is always a little too buttoned up and too close to their parents. They made reservations at the club at 8:00—is that too late? They kiss the lead actress on the cheek as they leave for work and she gives a small smile in return but already her heart belongs to the random stranger that she happened to run into at the park or Save the Puppies rally or during the emergency surprise earthquake that descended on San Francisco. The audience never feels too bad when the lead actress gives him back his ring and says, "We're just not right for each other, are we?" because he wasn't on the poster, so we knew not to care too much about him.

That's what dating Charlie is like. It's nice. It's safe. You're an altogether pleasant version of yourself but one who swallows her words sometimes and feels as though Something. Is. Missing. There is some symbolic version of soul mates that the screenwriter lazily inserted—knowing your favorite book is *The Little Prince*, wanting to share desserts—that he falls short on.

Now the wedding is in two weeks and all of the invitations have been sent out but what if he's not The One? Your free-spirited (perpetually single) friend tells you to follow your heart.

What's a leading lady to do?

A. Break up with him. Maybe Matt is still single. You can metaphorically run from the chapel (er, synagogue) into his arms (er, Twitter DMs), still wearing your wedding dress.

Turn to page 247.

B. Get married.

Turn to page 246.

SURPRISE! You live happily ever after, because you know that good relationship that's safe and content? Turns out that was a good relationship after all and the one that was built entirely on trickery and witty banter was incredibly toxic— good for a weekend of adventure maybe, but not an entire lifetime. Sure, Matthew McConaughey's come-what-may attitude seems charming now, but it won't in a year's time when he's an unemployed former surfing instructor with a beer belly masking his abs. Charlie, with the stable job, who loves you and gets along with your mom, is a supportive and warmhearted husband. The love that compelled you to agree to marry him in the first place wasn't diminished by that small bout of cold feet before the wedding when you thought that your charming neighbor played by Chris Evans might be your soul mate all along. Guess what? Soul mates don't exist. You build your own soul mate by committing to someone and working through the challenges that come from daily frustrations in every relationship, and that's the type of commitment that carries you and Charlie through a lifetime of laughter and mutual respect. You have three kids and eleven grandkids. You die within a week of each other.

THE END

YOU CHOOSE THE PLACE FOR YOUR FIRST DATE:
Johnny's Bar, right off 14th Street—a tiny dive that always
has seats and offers homemade pickle juice for their pickle-
backs. It's the only bar in the city you know to recommend.
He's taller than you imagined, and incredibly cute when he
smiles. You had gotten to the bar early and decided to pose
outside, one leg bent behind you, up against the wall so that
when he arrives he finds you casual and scrolling through
your phone. He was right on time.

This is just a plan B date, just a warm-up with someone
who seems nice enough. You're not expecting anything magical. You came straight from work, wearing a baggy sweater
and leggings. Your hair, which you hadn't had time to wash
the night before, is in a messy bun. Whatever drugstore
concealer and lip balm you had put on in the mirror that
morning had been wiped off by a day's worth of sweat and
napkins. He signed up online to date you, you tell yourself.
It doesn't matter how you look.

"Diet Coke, please," you say to the bartender when the
two of you claim your stools at the bar. He orders a beer.

Before he arrived, you'd already planned out your
evening: don't even get a drink, just a diet soda, so you don't
owe him even the price of an Old Fashioned and therefore
won't feel obligated to stick around any longer than you want
to.

"So," you say, swirling your legs around closer to him,
"what made you want to sign up to date a random stranger
online?" Despite pledging to play it cool, your flirting in-

stincts are coming out like an X-Men power you haven't learned to control. You are the Rogue of flirting. If a guy over six feet tall gets within touching distance of you, your body involuntarily begins to flirt. The government wants to put you on a registry.

"I've been following your tweets for a while," he says. "Mostly out of jealousy since we're the same age. Actually"— he takes a sip of his beer—"I think I saw you last summer at the Brooklyn Book Festival. I was interning at *Lapham's Quarterly* and working their booth. I recognized you from Twitter but I was too embarrassed to say anything."

A glow from your chest radiates through your entire body. "You should've said something!" you say lamely. He shrugs.

A half hour later, your legs are tangled with his. In five more minutes, you lean in and kiss him in the bar. "Do you want to take a walk?" you say.

You're halfway down the block before Matt stops. "What is it?"

"Shit," he says. "I forgot my backpack in the bar. I'll be right back!"

He dashes back into Johnny's and comes out with it slung over his shoulders, the tips of his ears burning red, visible even in the dark.

"I was distracted," he says, looking into your eyes and smiling. He's like the adorable protagonist from a romantic comedy, clumsy and lovestruck and totally into you. He's one prat fall away from being Justin Bartha. His hand grasps yours.

You walk around the block once, finally ducking into an archway of a church to make out, back to the stone, while he stands above you, grinning every time he pulls away.

"You wouldn't want to come back to my place to hang out some more, would you?" you ask.

"Yeah, I would like that a lot."

You smile and take his hand, leading the way to the subway. "Okay, but you have to promise me something. You have to promise if we sleep together on the first date you're not going to leave and then never speak to me again."

He looks at you like you're joking. "Dana, I would not do that. I like you."

The next day, the two of you text for hours. You barely look at your work computer because every time you finally focus, your phone dings an alert that this cute, funny, literary boy who seems to like you has sent you a message. You see each other the next day, and the day after that. Within a week, the two of you are boyfriend and girlfriend, and even that talk, the "what are we?" feels like a bygone conclusion, a hilarious formality you share out of tradition even though it was so obvious that this is someone you're meant to be with for as long as you can be.

One morning, he's brushing his teeth at your sink, and you're headed off to work, almost early for the first time since you were hired. "Bye," you say, whipping out the door, "I love you." You catch your step and pop back. "I mean, I don't love you. I really like you but, I was just, you know, 'goodbye, I love you!' as a whole thing, like one word. You know?"

"I know," he says, and grins.

That night, in the shower, he plops a handful of soap onto your left breast. "That thing you said this morning. I feel like it's just going to keep happening naturally. Next time, I think we can just probably go with it."

You try to hold eye contact. You can't say it first. "Hey," you say. "I really love spending time with you."

"I love spending time with you too."

You test the words in your mouth, like you're reading from a foreign language or testing out a secret password. "I love you," you say.

He grabs both your arms and looks right into your eyes.

"I love you, Dana."

He meets your parents and your little sister and he's very polite and looks nice in a button-down shirt. He brought you a Shirley Jackson collection he found at his office because you told him on your first date that your favorite book was *We Have Always Lived in the Castle*. He comes with you to the musical adaptation of *American Psycho* and you deconstruct it later, under your covers until you're both sneezing with laughter (the songs from the musical are stuck in your head for a solid six weeks). He goes out to brunch with your friends. You go to Christmas at his house. You help his little sister pick out a dog. Sometimes, you see him sleeping in bed, still wearing whatever button-down he was wearing the day before (Matt, it turns out, wears only regular clothes as pajamas). He'll be still asleep, but if you nudge his arm with your head, he'll reach over and scoop you into the nook of his body, and your two bodies will fit together so perfectly that you feel as though the slightest pressure will cause the spaces between your molecules to line up perfectly and condense the two of you into one. When you're under the comforter in the morning, and you see the lopsided succulent in the window, the succulent he went with you to buy when you were depressed and angry with the world and he stayed with you all day and helped you water your new succulent for the first time and it seemed so hopeful and perfect (even though your bedroom doesn't get enough natural light, and so the succulent began stretching and now it looks like a stalk of asparagus), and you feel his arm around you, you feel so lucky to get to feel as close to the real version of yourself you can ever be with another person. That's how it is sometimes. Sometimes it's ordinary, but it's usually the first feeling.

Your past comes back to you in a text message, innocuous and small, just a tiny series of letters on the screen you look at most of the day every day from a number in your phone that you never actually typed a name in for. Just a little blue bubble from a series of too-familiar numbers that says: "I miss you."

It's the easiest game in the world, a glimmering slot machine in a Vegas casino that lets you win every single time. Just write back. "I miss you too."

His reply: "I can't stop thinking about you."

The dialogue would be on the nose in a telenovela. But here you are, stopping on a city street before you make it into your office to reply.

"You know I can't stop thinking about you either." It's rote at this point, like delivering lines from a school play that you forget the context for, but the muscle memory of the words are permanently ready on your tongue. "Where are you?"

"Back in Austin. Cat is asleep on my legs."

You take a sharp inhale of breath.

"And your wife?" you text.

"She's at a conference this weekend. Home alone."

You don't reply, and so he writes again. You've moved to the edge of the sidewalk, back up against a Chipotle while the commuters of the financial district whiz past you in their khakis and brown shoes.

"I'm coming to New York next week. I'd really like to see you."

Before, it had only been him with the external risk factor, the wife, the ring, the promise he made. You had been testing to see how far he would go for you. Now you have a significant other too. You wonder if you love your boyfriend more than he loves his wife.

"I don't think that's such a good idea," you type back. You're not sure if you're feinting or not.

"We can just do coffee," he writes back. "Very chaste."

"Like we've ever managed to be chaste."

"Ha ha ha." Artificial typed laughter has never felt stranger than when he types it.

It's been two years since you've seen him. And even when you did see him, it'd only been three times in your life. But precocious college-aged seductress still feels like the role you were born to play.

"So, the coffee?"

What do you write back?

A. "Of course. I really want to see your face again. But just coffee."

Turn to page 253.

B. "I'm sorry. I'm sorry for leading you on now and before. I'm deleting your number and I think you should delete mine."

Turn to page 258.

COFFEE BECAME A HOTEL IN MIDTOWN, at 7:30 at night. "A bottle of champagne and I'm yours," you texted, half jokingly, while you were in the cab. You're wearing heels, and so you couldn't possibly walk.

"Done," he texted. "I'm on the champagne." He's very literal, and very serious, you realize. You never liked him for his sense of humor. More the way his hair curled over one eye and he spoke to you in a deep, raspy growl. And the way he seemed to be obsessed with you. You like that most of all, the gravitational pull between the two of you.

You check your cleavage in the front-facing camera of your phone and reapply your lipstick.

He said he'd meet you in the lobby and you check the address three times to make sure you're going to the right hotel, a big corporate place for businessmen and their conferences.

At first, you don't see him. But then you move farther, past the unattended piano and the pillars of the cavernous lobby, and there he is, wearing a button-up shirt with the top few buttons undone, smiling to see you.

You begin to move in for a kiss, but he pulls you in for a hug first, breathing you in deeply and then taking half a step back to just look at you.

"You look beautiful."

You fidget all the way up to his room, touching his hand and then pulling yours away, wondering if the people in the elevator know what's happening. You wish you'd worn less makeup.

He has champagne in his room, true to his word. "But I

could not, for the life of me, find champagne glasses in Midtown. We'll have to go with wineglasses."

He rinses the hotel's wineglasses and wipes their insides with a Kleenex, leaving a speckled residue of white bits that disappear when he pours the two glasses of champagne. "Cheers."

You take your glass, but you're sitting at the hotel room's desk, not on the bed. Your legs are crossed at the ankle. You had told Matt you were just having a quiet night at home and that you would see him tomorrow and that you loved him. You don't feel guilty so much as guilty that you're not all that attracted to Married Guy right this moment. Maybe it was the hotel, or how he got you champagne just because you asked. He wasn't quite as irresistible once he was there, in his hotel room, waiting for you to get undressed but he smells like you remember. And his eyes haven't left your body since they saw you.

The champagne glass is still full. You don't have much to say. "Hey," you start, and decide to come up with the end of the sentence as you go, but you can't think of anything and so instead you just kiss him and he kisses you back, a sloppy kiss that's somehow all mouth and no tongue and you kiss him back even harder and the two of you fall onto the bed and without even taking your underwear off he pulls it to the side and presses up against you and into you. Five minutes later your makeup is smudged in half-moons beneath your eyes and you want to go home.

"I'm going to go home," you say.

"It was good to see you," he says. "I'm back in New York in three weeks."

"You're still with your wife," you say, just as a fact, but he takes it as a question.

"Yes."

"You love her," you say.

"Yes."

You pull your shoes on and stuff your bra in your purse instead of putting it back on. "Think of me," you say.

"Oh, I will," he says. "More than I should."

Was it you who broke up with Matt or Matt who broke up with you? You weren't exactly hiding what you were doing— he saw it in the constant texts you were lingering over, the photos you scroll past in your phone that he knows you didn't send to him, the mediocre excuses. And when the confrontation came, tearfully on both sides, there was nothing to do but release the whole thing, like a boat pushed into the ocean. I love you, I'm sorry, I'm messed up, it wasn't your fault. He kisses you goodbye, which breaks your heart. You cry for two days and have to lock yourself out of your phone to keep yourself from texting him.

Married Guy comes back in three weeks, and you go to a small tapas restaurant he read about on the Lower East Side. When he leaves your place in the morning, he says he'll be back in a month, but then two days later, he texts you.

I don't think we can do this anymore. I want to work on my marriage.

The easy punch line to the maudlin opera you turned your life into. The prideful, lustful woman punished, the valiant heroes redeemed and rewarded with a happy ending in the form of a farmer's virtuous daughter. Let the woman in the red dress sing one last screeching aria and then die onstage before the happy wedding scenes.

But hey, you have a book coming out in the spring, a young adult novel with a blue-green cover with a faceless girl looking away, one hand flung into the air. "I full on cried when I got to the end," your sister confesses, and that's the only early review that truly makes you happy.

You interviewed for a new job, through a cavernous marble lobby and up a high-speed elevator into the modern, open-floor plan offices of the *New York Observer*.

"Your voice would be perfect for our arts and culture vertical," Drew says, talking fast. She has short dyed hair, and she's wearing cutoff jeans. A watercolor tattoo disappears into her sleeve. "Honestly, from the minute I read your stuff, I was like, one, this girl reminds me of me, and two, I need her to write for me in the meantime. The thing about the *Observer* is there's a ton of freedom and flexibility. And the access is amazing. You can basically interview whoever you want."

"That sounds amazing," you agree. You never imagined that you would be an actual arts and culture writer, but, you realize, movies and TV shows are what you spend most of your time thinking about and ranting about and tweeting about. You have opinions and ideas. And getting to spend your days interviewing famous people and critiquing movies and making jokes on the Internet seems like the best thing in the world. You think about everything in terms of movie tropes and now someone will pay you for it.

"So yeah," Drew continues. "I already talked to our editor in chief, and he loves your stuff. That *Real Housewives* piece you wrote was *hilarious*. It's literally exactly what we're trying to do with the *Observer* brand right now. Smart and snarky. So, do you have any questions for me?"

"Is there ever any weirdness with...Jared Kushner owning the paper?" you ask. Last week, the *Observer* endorsed Donald Trump in the Republican primary. The food critic had publicly resigned over it.

Drew shifted slightly and exhaled. "Honestly, you never see or deal with him. The amazing thing about the Arts and Culture vertical is we have complete autonomy. I'm not sure what the situation is like in Politics, but no one cares what sort of thing you're writing about. And the only way you'd ever have to write anything about Donald Trump is if *The Apprentice* is renewed for another season." She leans forward conspiratorially. "I mean, everyone who actually works in the office is super liberal. Plus, there's no actual way he's going to win, so yeah, it's been kind of weird but basically the idea is we just get through November or even...when's the Republican primary again? Get through that, he loses, everyone forgets about him and Kushner and then things get back to normal."

The next day, the editor in chief calls and offers you the job, to start as soon as you can. You take a day, and then accept. There are business cards with your name sitting on your desk on your first day, black matte on one side and your name on the other:

DANA SCHWARTZ
ARTS AND CULTURE WRITER

So here you are, single and working and living in New York City. All you can do is let every other version of yourself fall away like an exoskeleton and then start over.

THE END

HE DOESN'T RESPOND. He never responds. You, feeling like the protagonist in an after-school TV special, delete his number from your phone. You take the shame of his flattery and the songs you sent him and the photographs you sent him and the "I love yous" and thigh touches and put them away somewhere packed neatly in the back of your brain where you keep Civil War facts from elementary school and the good china.

You tell Matt that your ex had messaged you, the married one, from college, that he wanted to meet you for coffee. You told him what you texted back, the whole "I think you should delete mine too" line, and showed him a screen shot because you're not quite sure if he'd believe you otherwise.

You're not a better person than you were when you were nineteen. You're still hungry for affection and desperately lonely. You still push relationships too quickly, scared people will leave you if they aren't bound by blood or promises spoken and repeated a hundred times. You still eat full pints of ice cream whenever you buy them in a single sitting. Your room has never been clean for longer than four hours. But you deleted his number. You have a job, and a place to live, and a boyfriend who's able to love you back.

Whoever you want to be, just start here and be her now. Every day you get to start again.

THE END

ACKNOWLEDGMENTS

Thank you so much to all of the incredible people who helped me turn this objectively insane and ill-advised project into reality. First, as always, I need to thank my family for their undying support and love in the face of the endless embarrassing things I do: Caroline, who was the first person to read this book and who understood that we needed to prevent our parents from reading it; Hallie, whom I will happily admit is funnier than I am, and who is always willing to teach me how to take photos for Instagram; Zach, who has been my debating partner for life; and Mom and Dad, who have always let me fearlessly pursue my dreams by letting me know that I had a safe place to fall.

To Matt, who made me feel more loved than I knew I was allowed.

Thank you to my tireless agent, Dan Mandel, for everything he's done for me in my life and career, for making me feel confident enough to sell books and then sane enough to write them, and for always answering my rambling, middle-of-the-night emails in a timely fashion.

To my fearless editor, Maddie Caldwell, and the entire

Grand Central team, I will never be able to thank you enough for your faith in this book and everything you did to make it something I could be proud of. You are wise and patient and incredibly good at your jobs.

To Drew and Vinnie at the *Observer*, for all of their patience and help as I attempted to write a book while also writing full-time, usually about *The OA*.

To Neil, for answering my panicked messages and offering preternaturally wise advice. You are an inspiration in work and in life.

To Hannah and Natalie and Jason and Max and Kat and Simon and Jennifer and Daniel for their friendship and love and patience.

To all of the men I've slept with, thank you for giving me what I needed in that moment, for making me feel special or wanted or loved. And if you hurt me, thank you for helping me to learn while I was young. Hope you bought this book full price just to see if I wrote about you.